BY

Dan Claassen

It is creative nonfiction, in this case. For various reasons, several parts have undergone variable degrees of fictionalization.

# Table of Contents

# Introduction

In a world full of possibilities, "Sales-Driven Lifestyle" reveals the transformative impact of sales on all aspects of our lives. Explore how effective communication skills can revolutionize relationships, elevate salesmanship, and deepen personal connections.

Discover the art of persuasion, active listening, and negotiation secrets to navigate challenges and seize opportunities in both professional and personal spheres. Embrace the harmonious balance between a sales-oriented career and personal life, unlocking the full potential of sales to improve finances and navigate successful job searches.

Gain insights into the entrepreneurial mindset, forge meaningful relationships, conquer fear and self-doubt, and set and achieve personal goals with determination. Explore the intersection of sales and marketing, understand the customer lifecycle, and embrace personal branding. Learn to maintain work-life balance, experience the fulfilment of philanthropy, and unlock a more empowered and fulfilling everyday life.

Let "Sales-Driven Lifestyle" guide you to lead a life enriched by meaningful connections, personal growth, and a sales-driven mentality.

# Chapter 1: Understanding Sales as a Part of Your Everyday Life

Sales is a complex and ever-present part of our daily existence, involving a lot more than just traditional business transactions. It is the art of persuasion, effective communication, and the ability to influence others in various personal and professional contexts. By gaining a deeper understanding of sales and its impact, we can navigate our lives more effectively and achieve favorable outcomes.

Sales extend beyond financial transactions, infiltrating our daily interactions, choices, and decision-making processes. Whether we realize it or not, we engage in numerous sales-related exchanges. Imagine a situation where you're trying to convince a friend to join you for a movie. You describe the movie's thrilling plot, talented actors, and rave reviews to persuade your friend to accompany you. In this scenario, you are utilizing sales techniques to influence their decision. Similarly, negotiating vacation plans with family members involves sales where you seek a compromise that satisfies everyone involved.

The power of sales lies in its ability to influence decisions, regardless of the context. Whether convincing a colleague to support your idea during a meeting or persuading your child to complete their homework, understanding sales principles can significantly impact the outcome. Effective communication, empathetic understanding, and presenting compelling solutions increase the likelihood of influencing decisions in our favor. Sales play a crucial role in building and nurturing relationships.

Successful salespeople prioritize establishing long-term connections based on trust, mutual understanding, and shared value. Similarly, in our personal lives, forging strong relationships requires connecting with others, establishing trust, and comprehending their needs. This process entails practicing empathy, actively listening, and communicating effectively.

Self-presentation and personal branding are vital aspects of sales. How we present ourselves influences others' perceptions and decisions. Like sales professionals creating personal brands that resonate with their target audience, we shape our brand daily. Whether attending a job interview, networking at a social event, or even engaging on social media platforms, we continually project ourselves in ways that influence how others perceive us.

To thrive in sales-driven interactions, certain skills prove invaluable. Empathy plays a critical role in building connections and fostering positive relationships. By placing ourselves in others' shoes, we can comprehend their needs, address their concerns, and find common ground. Adopting a sales mindset involves cultivating a proactive and solution-oriented approach to life. It means viewing challenges as opportunities for growth. Embracing this mindset empowers us to navigate personal and professional situations with confidence, adaptability, and resilience.

The sales mindset encourages seeking win-win outcomes, prioritizing relationships, and striving for continuous improvement. It provides a comprehensive understanding of sales as an integral part of our everyday lives. It expands our perception of sales beyond traditional transactions and highlights its influence in decision-making, relationship-building, self-presentation, and personal branding.

By recognizing the pervasive nature of sales and developing essential sales skills, we can navigate our lives with greater success and fulfilment. Sales permeate every facet of our daily existence, encompassing various interactions and decisions that shape our personal and professional lives. It is more than mere transactions: the art of persuasion, effective communication, and the ability to influence others in various contexts.

While we may not always recognize it, we engage in sales-related activities regularly. From convincing a friend to join us for an outing to negotiating with family members, we employ sales techniques to sway opinions and achieve desired outcomes. The influence of sales extends beyond financial matters, affecting decision-making processes across diverse areas of life. Whether we are persuading a colleague to support our ideas or encouraging our children to complete tasks, understanding sales principles can greatly enhance our ability to influence others. We can increase the likelihood of achieving favorable outcomes by effectively communicating our thoughts, empathizing with others, and presenting compelling solutions.

Sales also play a pivotal role in building and maintaining relationships. Successful salespeople prioritize establishing long-term connections based on trust, understanding, and shared values. Similarly, in our personal lives, connecting with others, building trust, and empathizing with their needs are essential for cultivating meaningful relationships. How we present ourselves and manage our brand is a crucial aspect of sales.

Our appearance, communication style, and online presence shape others' perceptions and influence the decisions they make about us. As sales professionals carefully craft their brand to resonate with their target audience, we continually shape it in various social and professional settings. To thrive in sales-driven interactions, developing and refining specific skills is crucial. Empathy is another key skill allowing us to relate to others, comprehend their needs, and address their concerns.

By adopting a proactive and solution-oriented mindset, we can navigate personal and professional situations with confidence and resilience. Embracing a sales mindset involves viewing challenges as opportunities for growth and constantly seeking ways to add value to others.

It means prioritizing relationships, seeking win-win outcomes, and continuously improving ourselves. By adopting this mindset, we can enhance our ability to influence decisions, build stronger relationships, and achieve greater personal and professional fulfilment.

# Chapter 2: Why Embracing a Sales Mindset Has Benefits Beyond Your Career

Embracing a sales mindset goes beyond its applications in the realm of business. It is a mindset that can benefit all aspects of our lives. Understanding and adopting sales principles can enhance our relationships, improve communication skills, and navigate challenges with greater confidence and success. At its core, a sales mindset is rooted in persuasion and influence.

This mindset empowers us to build rapport, establish trust, and connect more deeply with people from all walks of life. One of the key benefits of embracing a sales mindset is the improvement of our communication skills. Effective communication is a cornerstone of successful sales and is pivotal in our personal and professional interactions. Strong communication skills allow us to express our thoughts and ideas clearly, actively listen to others, and understand their perspectives.

This leads to better understanding, fewer misunderstandings, and more harmonious relationships. A sales mindset also fosters a proactive and solution-oriented approach to challenges. Instead of seeing obstacles as roadblocks, we view them as opportunities for growth and problem-solving. This mindset encourages us to think creatively, explore different options, and find win-win solutions that benefit all parties involved. It empowers us to overcome setbacks, adapt to change, and embrace new opportunities enthusiastically.

Embracing a sales mindset cultivates resilience and a positive attitude. Sales professionals understand that rejection and setbacks are part of the journey. They develop the ability to bounce back, learn from their experiences, and persist in adversity. This resilience translates into our personal lives as well. We become more adept at handling rejection, navigating challenges, and maintaining a positive outlook even in difficult times. The practice of empathy is another significant aspect of a sales mindset. Empathy allows us to put ourselves in others' shoes, understand their emotions and perspectives, and respond with compassion and understanding.

Empathizing with others can build deeper connections, resolve conflicts more effectively, and foster harmonious relationships. Embracing a sales mindset can transform our relationships and make them more fulfilling. It enables us to communicate our needs, listen attentively to the needs of others, and find common ground. Adopting a sales mindset allows us to navigate conflicts, negotiate compromises, and build stronger bonds with our loved ones.

This approach fosters understanding, open communication, and mutual respect, leading to healthier and more satisfying relationships. A sales mindset can have a positive impact on our overall well-being. It promotes a sense of purpose and motivation as we strive to add value to the lives of others.

By focusing on helping and serving others, we experience a deep sense of fulfilment and satisfaction. This mindset also encourages continuous learning and personal growth as we seek to refine our skills, expand our knowledge, and stay updated with the latest trends and insights. Embracing a sales mindset offers numerous benefits beyond our careers. It enhances our communication skills, encourages a proactive and solution-oriented approach to challenges, fosters resilience and a positive attitude, and cultivates empathy and stronger personal relationships.

By adopting a sales mindset, we can navigate life with greater confidence, connect with others on a deeper level, and lead more fulfilling and successful lives. Embracing a sales mindset transcends the boundaries of traditional business contexts and extends into various aspects of our lives. Adopting this mindset unlocks many benefits that positively impact our well-being, relationships, and success. One significant advantage of embracing a sales mindset is the development of effective persuasion skills.

Sales professionals understand the art of influencing others, and by incorporating this mindset into our everyday lives, we can hone our ability to communicate our ideas, opinions, and desires persuasively. This skill allows us to navigate social dynamics, negotiate compromises, and gain buy-in from others, leading to more favorable outcomes in personal interactions and decision-making processes.

A sales mindset also encourages continuous self-improvement and a growth-oriented approach. Sales professionals constantly seek ways to refine their techniques, expand their knowledge, and adapt to changing circumstances. Similarly, when we embrace a sales mindset, we become more open to feedback, willing to learn from our experiences, and eager to explore new strategies for personal growth. A sales mindset instils a proactive attitude towards problem-solving. Rather than succumbing to challenges, we are empowered to approach them as puzzles to be solved. This mindset encourages us to think creatively, consider alternative perspectives, and explore innovative solutions.

By adopting a sales mindset, we become adept at identifying opportunities within obstacles and finding win-win resolutions for ourselves and others. This proactive approach builds resilience, fosters adaptability, and strengthens our ability to overcome adversity. An essential aspect of a sales mind is cultivating strong interpersonal skills. Sales professionals recognize the importance of building rapport, establishing trust, and fostering client relationships. When we embrace this mindset in our personal lives, we become more attuned to the needs and emotions of others.

We develop active listening skills, which enable us to genuinely understand others' perspectives, empathize with their experiences, and respond with compassion and understanding. These enhanced interpersonal skills contribute to deeper and more meaningful connections, enriching our personal relationships and overall well-being.

Moreover, a sales mindset encourages a focus on creating value for others. Sales professionals understand that successful sales are built on the principle of delivering meaningful solutions that meet the needs of their customers. When we adopt this mindset, we become more attuned to the needs of those around us, whether our friends, family members, or colleagues.

By actively seeking ways to add value to their lives, we strengthen our relationships, build trust, and foster a sense of reciprocity. This approach benefits others and brings us a sense of purpose and fulfilment. In addition to its impact on personal relationships, embracing a sales mindset can extend to our broader communities.

Sales professionals often engage in philanthropic activities, using their skills to raise awareness and funds for causes they believe in. By incorporating this mindset into our lives, we can leverage our persuasive abilities and influence to impact society positively. Whether volunteering our time, supporting local initiatives, or championing important social causes, we can use sales principles to drive meaningful change and contribute to the greater good.

Embracing a sales mindset offers many benefits that extend far beyond our careers. It equips us with effective persuasion skills, encourages a growth-oriented approach to personal development, fosters proactive problem-solving abilities, enhances interpersonal skills, promotes a focus on creating value for others, and enables us to impact our communities positively.

Adopting a sales mindset unlocks our potential for personal growth, stronger relationships, and a more meaningful and successful life.

# Chapter 3: Communication Skills That Improve Sales and Personal Relationships

Effective communication is a cornerstone of successful sales and is pivotal in fostering strong personal relationships. By honing our communication skills, we can enhance our ability to connect with others, convey our ideas, and build rapport.

Effective communication is essential for establishing understanding, resolving conflicts, and nurturing meaningful connections, whether in a sales context or our lives.

One fundamental aspect of communication is the art of active listening. Sales professionals understand the importance of listening to clients to uncover their needs, concerns, and desires. Active listening allows us to understand and empathize with the people in our lives truly. It involves giving our full attention, maintaining eye contact, and demonstrating genuine interest in what the other person is saying.

By actively listening, we create a safe space for open dialogue, show respect, and build trust, leading to stronger connections and more productive interactions.

Effective communication requires clarity and conciseness. Professionals aim to articulate their value propositions clearly and succinctly when engaging in sales conversations. This same principle applies to personal relationships. By expressing our thoughts, feelings, and expectations clearly and concisely, we minimize misunderstandings and ensure our message is accurately received.

Choosing words carefully is important using appropriate tone and body language, and confidently conveying our message. The clarity in communication allows for effective problem-solving, efficient decision-making, and the cultivation of mutual understanding. Another vital skill is adapting our communication style to suit different individuals and situations.

Sales professionals are adept at tailoring their approach to match their clients' preferences and communication styles. Understanding and adapting to the communication preferences of our loved ones can greatly enhance our connections. Some individuals prefer direct and assertive communication, while others may respond better to a more empathetic and supportive approach.

Flexibility and adjusting our communication style can ensure effective communication and build stronger, more harmonious relationships. Emotional intelligence is also crucial for effective communication in both sales and personal relationships. It involves recognizing and understanding our own emotions and those of others.

Sales professionals leverage emotional intelligence to connect with their clients on a deeper level and respond appropriately to their needs and concerns. In our personal lives, emotional intelligence allows us to navigate conflicts, show empathy, and support the emotional well-being of those around us.

Sales professionals understand the importance of maintaining positive body language and projecting confidence during client interactions. Likewise, in personal relationships, nonverbal cues convey messages that can either enhance or hinder communication.

Being mindful of our body language, maintaining eye contact, and using appropriate gestures can enhance our message's impact and ensure that our intentions align with our words. Nonverbal communication provides additional layers of meaning and can reinforce trust and understanding between individuals.

Effective communication requires active feedback and continuous improvement. Sales professionals actively seek feedback from their clients to gauge their satisfaction.

Similarly, seeking and providing feedback is vital for ongoing growth and understanding in personal relationships. By encouraging open dialogue, being receptive to constructive criticism, and actively enhancing our communication skills, we can continuously improve our ability to connect with others and foster stronger relationships. Effective communication is a critical skill that benefits both sales and personal relationships.

Active listening, clarity, adaptability, emotional intelligence, nonverbal communication, and feedback contribute to successful communication. Developing these skills allows us to establish understanding, resolve conflicts, and build trust in our interactions. Effective communication is key to fostering meaningful connections and achieving positive sales or personal relationship outcomes.

Effective communication is a powerful tool for improving sales outcomes and nurturing personal relationships. Let's explore additional facets of communication skills that can further enhance these areas of our lives. One crucial aspect of communication is the ability to convey empathy and understanding.

Sales professionals recognize the importance of putting themselves in their client's shoes to comprehend their needs and concerns fully. Similarly, empathetic communication allows us to connect with others more deeply in personal relationships.

By actively seeking to understand and validate the emotions and experiences of our loved ones, we create an atmosphere of trust and support. Empathetic communication involves actively listening, acknowledging feelings, and responding with compassion. It enables us to build stronger bonds and develop mutual understanding.

Another vital communication skill is the art of storytelling. Sales professionals often utilize storytelling techniques to captivate their audience and convey the value of their products. In personal relationships, storytelling can be equally impactful.

Sharing personal anecdotes, experiences, and narratives allows us to connect more intimately. It creates a shared sense of vulnerability and fosters a deeper connection with others. We can enhance our communication and strengthen relationships by employing storytelling techniques, such as engaging narratives, vivid descriptions, and relatable experiences.

Conflict resolution is another critical aspect of effective communication. Conflicts may arise when dealing with demanding clients or negotiating challenging situations in sales. Navigating conflicts and reaching satisfactory resolutions is essential for maintaining positive client relationships.

Conflicts are a natural part of personal relationships, and how we handle them can determine the strength and longevity of those connections. By employing active listening, empathy, and open-mindedness, we can approach conflicts with a collaborative mindset, seeking solutions that consider the needs and perspectives of all parties involved.

Effective communication during conflict resolution promotes understanding, facilitates compromise, and preserves the integrity of the relationships. Cultivating assertiveness is also important in both sales and personal relationships.

Sales professionals must confidently express their value propositions, negotiate terms, and address objections. Assertiveness is vital in personal relationships to express our boundaries, preferences, and needs. By asserting ourselves respectfully and assertively, we ensure that our voice is heard, our opinions are considered, and our contributions are valued.

Assertive communication promotes honesty, transparency, and mutual respect in our interactions, ultimately strengthening our relationships and allowing for more open and authentic connections. The skill of nonverbal communication goes beyond body language and encompasses other subtle cues, such as tone of voice, facial expressions, and gestures.

Sales professionals understand the impact of nonverbal communication in building trust and establishing rapport with clients. In personal relationships, nonverbal cues are crucial in understanding emotions, intentions, and underlying messages.

Being attuned to nonverbal signals allows us to interpret others' feelings better and respond accordingly. It also helps us effectively convey our emotions, ensuring our verbal and nonverbal communication aligns.

By honing our nonverbal communication skills, we can create an atmosphere of understanding, authenticity, and emotional connection in sales and personal relationships. Adapting our communication to different platforms and mediums is another valuable skill in today's interconnected world.

To engage with clients effectively, sales professionals are adept at utilizing various communication channels, such as email, phone calls, and video conferencing.

# Chapter 4: The Power of Active Listening in Both Sales and Personal Life

Active listening is a transformative skill with immense power in sales interactions and personal relationships. It goes beyond simply hearing words and involves fully engaging with the speaker, understanding their message, and responding empathetically.

By practicing active listening, we can forge deeper connections, uncover valuable insights, and foster harmonious communication. In sales, active listening is a fundamental tool for understanding clients' needs, preferences, and pain points. It allows sales professionals to gather crucial information that helps them tailor their offerings and provide personalized solutions.

By actively listening to their clients, salespeople demonstrate respect and genuine interest, building trust and rapport. This deep understanding enables them to address concerns effectively and position their products or services as valuable solutions. Through active listening, sales professionals can establish long-lasting customer relationships based on mutual trust and satisfaction. Active listening plays a pivotal role in personal relationships.

When we practice active listening with our loved ones, friends, and acquaintances, we demonstrate our willingness to invest time and effort in understanding them. It involves giving our full attention, maintaining eye contact, and being present. We create a safe space for open and honest communication by focusing on the speaker and suspending judgment.

Active listening allows us to empathize with the speaker's emotions, validate their experiences, and strengthen our emotional bond. It nurtures a sense of being heard, valued, and understood, crucial for building healthy and meaningful relationships. One aspect of active listening is paraphrasing or summarizing the speaker's words. By restating or summarizing what we have heard, we confirm our understanding and allow the speaker to clarify any misconceptions. This technique helps us ensure accurate comprehension and shows the speaker that we are actively engaged and invested in the conversation.

Paraphrasing helps us remember and retain information, allowing for more meaningful follow-up discussions. This technique enables sales professionals to demonstrate their understanding of the client's needs and effectively present tailored solutions. In personal relationships, paraphrasing fosters clarity and ensures that both parties are on the same page, preventing misunderstandings and conflicts.

Nonverbal cues are an integral part of active listening. Sales professionals are trained to pay attention to their client's body language, facial expressions, and tone of voice to gauge their engagement, interest, and emotional state. In personal relationships, nonverbal cues provide valuable insights into the speaker's emotions and intentions. By observing and interpreting nonverbal cues, such as facial expressions, gestures, and posture, we can better understand the speaker's underlying feelings and respond appropriately. Being attuned to nonverbal cues allows us to connect more profoundly and establish emotional connections and trust.

Active listening also involves asking thoughtful and relevant questions. By asking open-ended questions, we encourage the speaker to elaborate and share more information. This demonstrates our interest and allows us to gather valuable insights and perspectives. In sales, asking probing questions helps sales professionals uncover hidden objections or concerns that might impact the buying decision. In personal relationships, asking open-ended questions allows us to delve deeper into the thoughts, emotions, and experiences of our loved ones.

Thoughtful questioning fosters meaningful conversations and encourages speakers to reflect on their perspectives and insights. Another crucial aspect of active listening is avoiding distractions and being fully present in the conversation. In today's fast-paced world, distractions abound, from buzzing smartphones to wandering thoughts.

We show respect and prioritize the conversation by consciously eliminating distractions and focusing on the speaker. Being present allows us to absorb information, notice subtle nuances, and respond genuinely. In sales, this level of presence enables sales professionals to pick up on key client cues and tailor their approach accordingly.

Being fully present demonstrates our commitment and investment in the relationship in personal relationships, leading to more fulfilling and authentic connections. It requires conscious effort and a genuine desire to understand and connect with others. We can transform our sales interactions and personal relationships by honing our active listening skills. We can build trust, gain valuable insights, and foster harmonious communication. Active listening involves suspending judgment and avoiding interrupting the speaker.

This practice allows for a free flow of ideas and encourages the speaker to share their thoughts openly. By refraining from interrupting, we respect the speaker's perspective and create an atmosphere of trust and collaboration. This approach helps sales professionals gather comprehensive information and understand clients' needs holistically. Personal relationships foster a sense of validation and encourage open and honest communication. Active listening involves being aware of our own biases and assumptions. It requires us to approach conversations with an open mind and be willing to challenge our preconceived notions.

We can truly listen and appreciate different perspectives by acknowledging and setting aside our biases. This practice is particularly valuable in sales, allowing sales professionals to adapt their approach and solutions to meet diverse client needs. It helps us to understand others' viewpoints and cultivate empathy and understanding. Active listening also encompasses providing feedback and validation to the speaker.

By offering genuine feedback, we demonstrate that we have listened to and understood the speaker's message. Feedback can take the form of affirmations, reflections, or constructive comments. It shows that we are engaged in the conversation and committed to mutual understanding. In sales, providing feedback can help sales professionals clarify client requirements, address concerns, and reinforce the value of their offerings.

Feedback promotes healthy communication, reinforces emotional connection, and strengthens individual bonds in personal relationships. Active listening extends beyond individual conversations and involves being mindful of the broader context. It means paying attention to the speaker's emotions, concerns, and aspirations in the present moment and the larger scope of their experiences.

By considering the context, we better understand the speaker's motivations, challenges, and desires. This comprehensive perspective allows us to respond with empathy and compassion. Understanding the broader context helps sales professionals tailor their approach and solutions to align with the client's goals and values.

Being mindful of the context in personal relationships allows us to support and empathize with our loved ones more meaningfully and positively. It involves responding thoughtfully and articulately to the speaker's messages. By offering well-considered responses, we show that we have not only listened but also internalized and reflected upon what has been shared.

This type of communication allows sales professionals to address client concerns, provide relevant information, and build trust. In personal relationships, it helps us engage in meaningful conversations, contribute to ongoing dialogue, and nurture the relationship through effective communication. Active listening is a powerful skill that transcends both sales and personal life. By actively listening, we demonstrate respect, empathy, and genuine interest in the speaker. This skill enables us to gather valuable information, understand diverse perspectives, and build strong connections.

Active listening involves paraphrasing, observing nonverbal cues, asking thoughtful questions, avoiding distractions, suspending judgment, being aware of biases, providing feedback, considering the context, and responding effectively.

By incorporating active listening into our daily interactions, we can enhance our sales success and the quality of our relationships.

# Chapter 5: Negotiation Skills That Can Help in Your Personal Life

Negotiation is a skill that goes beyond the realm of business and sales. It is a valuable tool that can also greatly benefit us personally. We can navigate conflicts, reach mutually beneficial agreements, and build stronger relationships by developing effective negotiation skills. Negotiation is all about finding common ground and reaching compromises that satisfy the interests of all parties involved. Conflicts and disagreements are inevitable in personal life, whether deciding on household responsibilities, making plans with friends, or resolving differences with loved ones.

The ability to negotiate allows us to address these conflicts constructively and find solutions that meet everyone's needs. One of the key elements of successful negotiation is effective communication. Expressing our perspectives, needs, and concerns is crucial in resolving them. It involves active listening to understand the other party's point of view and responding thoughtfully and respectfully. By fostering open and honest communication, we create an environment where negotiations can occur productively and respectfully. Another important aspect of negotiation is the ability to identify and prioritize interests. Instead of focusing solely on positions or demands, we should strive to understand all parties' underlying interests and motivations.

We can explore creative solutions that satisfy everyone involved by identifying shared interests. This collaborative approach fosters a sense of cooperation and encourages win-win outcomes. Negotiation also requires the skill of problem-solving. It involves analyzing the situation, brainstorming solutions, and evaluating their feasibility and impact.

By adopting a problem-solving mindset, we can explore alternative options and find innovative solutions that address the interests of all parties. This approach leads to better outcomes and strengthens relationships by demonstrating our commitment to finding mutually beneficial solutions. Emotional intelligence plays a significant role in negotiation, both in business and personal settings.

Being aware of and managing our emotions effectively allows us to navigate tense situations and maintain a calm and composed demeanor. Additionally, understanding and empathizing with the emotions of others helps us build rapport and find common ground. By considering the emotional aspects of negotiation, we can foster a positive and constructive atmosphere that facilitates agreement.

Negotiation often involves compromise. It requires us to be flexible and willing to make concessions to reach an agreement. However, compromising does not mean sacrificing our own needs or values. Instead, it involves finding creative solutions that address the interests of all parties involved. By seeking mutually beneficial outcomes, we can preserve relationships and build trust.

Trust is a vital element in negotiation. Building and maintaining trust requires honesty, integrity, and reliability. Trust allows parties to negotiate, knowing their interests will be respected and their agreements honored confidently. In personal relationships, trust forms the foundation for strong and lasting bonds. We can strengthen our connections and foster deeper relationships by demonstrating trustworthiness in our negotiations.

Negotiation skills also encompass the ability to manage and resolve conflicts. Conflict resolution involves understanding the root causes of disagreements, facilitating open dialogue, and finding common ground. By adopting a collaborative approach and seeking win-win solutions, we can turn conflicts into opportunities for growth and understanding. Effective conflict resolution enhances personal relationships by promoting understanding, empathy, and compromise.

Negotiation skills can be particularly valuable when making important decisions together in personal relationships. Whether deciding on major purchases, planning vacations, or choosing a course of action, effective negotiation allows all parties to have a voice and actively participate in decision-making. By engaging in constructive dialogue and considering different perspectives, we can find solutions considering everyone's needs and preferences. Negotiation skills can be beneficial in resolving conflicts that arise in personal relationships.

Disagreements and misunderstandings are a natural part of any relationship, but how we navigate and resolve them can make a significant difference. The ability to negotiate allows us to approach conflicts with empathy, patience, and a willingness to find common ground. By focusing on finding win-win solutions, we can address the underlying issues and maintain the strength and harmony of the relationship. Negotiation skills also come into play when managing interpersonal dynamics and addressing power imbalances.

Ensuring all parties feel heard, respected, and valued in personal relationships. We can foster a sense of equality and fairness by using negotiation techniques such as active listening, seeking mutual understanding, and promoting equitable decision-making. This strengthens individual bonds and creates a healthier and more balanced dynamic. Negotiation skills can be instrumental in setting and maintaining healthy boundaries in personal relationships. Boundaries help define acceptable and unacceptable behavior, personal space, and emotional needs. Through negotiation, we can establish boundaries that reflect our individual preferences and communicate them effectively to others. This promotes mutual understanding, respect, and safety within the relationship.

Negotiation skills also empower us to navigate challenging conversations and manage difficult emotions. There may be instances where we need to address sensitive topics, express our needs, or provide constructive feedback. We can navigate these conversations with compassion and understanding by applying negotiation techniques such as empathy, active listening, and clear communication. This helps create an atmosphere of openness and trust, fostering deeper connections and promoting personal growth.

Moreover, negotiation skills can be invaluable in managing external relationships beyond our immediate circle. Negotiation allows us to advocate for our needs and find mutually agreeable solutions, whether dealing with neighbors, community organizations, or other social interactions. By approaching these interactions with diplomacy, flexibility, and a willingness to collaborate, we can establish positive and harmonious relationships within our broader social networks.

Negotiation skills can be applied to personal goal-setting and self-advocacy. By understanding our needs, values, and aspirations, we can negotiate with ourselves to establish realistic goals and create action plans to achieve them. This self-negotiation process involves considering various options, assessing potential obstacles, and finding strategies to overcome them. We can enhance our personal growth, self-empowerment, and overall well-being by effectively negotiating with ourselves.

Negotiation skills have significant relevance and benefits in our personal lives. We can easily navigate personal relationships and create mutually satisfying outcomes by applying effective communication, understanding interests, problem-solving, practicing emotional intelligence, seeking compromise, building trust, resolving conflicts, and setting boundaries.

Negotiation empowers us to address conflicts, make important decisions, manage power dynamics, establish healthy boundaries, navigate challenging conversations, manage external relationships, and achieve personal goals. By honing these skills, we can foster stronger connections, enhance personal well-being, and cultivate fulfilling relationships.

# Chapter 6: How Your Sales Skills Can Benefit Your Non-Sales Job

Sales skills are valuable in sales-specific roles and have wide-ranging benefits in non-sales jobs. The ability to effectively communicate, build relationships, and influence others is highly transferable and can enhance your performance and success in various professional settings. Let's explore how your sales skills can benefit your non-sales job.

✓ Communication: Sales professionals excel in communication, which is crucial in any job. Effective communication involves articulating ideas clearly, actively listening to others, and adapting your message to different audiences. By leveraging your sales communication skills, you can effectively convey information, collaborate with colleagues, and engage with stakeholders. Clear communication facilitates understanding, minimizes misunderstandings, and enhances overall productivity.

✓ Relationship Building: Salespeople are skilled at building rapport and establishing client trust. These relationship-building abilities can be invaluable in non-sales roles as well. By nurturing positive relationships with colleagues, superiors, and clients, you can foster collaboration, gain support for your ideas, and create a harmonious work environment. Building strong relationships also opens doors to new opportunities, referrals, and valuable connections that can contribute to your professional growth.

✓ Persuasion and Influence: Sales professionals are adept at persuading others and influencing their decisions. This ability is not limited to selling products or services but can be applied in various work scenarios. Whether you need to persuade your team to adopt a new strategy, convince stakeholders of the value of your project, or negotiate for resources, your sales skills can help you present compelling arguments, address objections, and ultimately gain buy-in from others.

✓ Customer Focus: Salespeople have a customer-centric mindset, constantly striving to understand and meet customer needs. This customer focus is highly relevant in non-sales roles as well. This insight allows you to tailor your solutions, deliver exceptional service, and exceed expectations, leading to increased satisfaction and stronger relationships.

✓ Goal Orientation: Sales professionals are accustomed to setting and pursuing ambitious goals. This goal-oriented mindset can be applied in non-sales jobs to drive performance and achieve desired outcomes. By setting clear objectives, breaking them into actionable steps, and measuring progress, you can enhance productivity, maintain focus, and deliver results in your non-sales role. This proactive approach demonstrates your commitment to excellence and can position you for advancement opportunities.

✓ Problem-Solving: Salespeople encounter various challenges and are skilled at finding creative solutions. This problem-solving ability is highly transferable to non-sales jobs where critical thinking and analytical skills are valued. By leveraging your sales experience, you can approach complex problems with a structured and systematic mindset, identify alternative solutions, and make informed decisions. Your ability to navigate obstacles and find innovative solutions can set you apart in your non-sales role.

✓     Adaptability and Resilience: Sales professionals operate in a dynamic and competitive environment that demands adaptability and resilience. These qualities are highly sought-after in non-sales roles as well. By drawing on your experience in sales, you can demonstrate your ability to embrace change, remain calm under pressure, and quickly adapt to new circumstances. Your resilience allows you to persevere through challenges, maintain a positive attitude, and inspire others in your non-sales job.

✓     Data Analysis and Research: To inform their strategies, sales professionals often analyze market trends, customer data, and competitor information. This analytical mindset can be valuable in non-sales roles that involve data analysis and research. Applying your sales skills lets you gather and interpret data, identify patterns and insights, and make data-driven decisions in your non-sales job. This ability to leverage data effectively enhances your problem-solving capabilities and contributes to informed decision-making.

Your sales skills can potentially benefit your non-sales job significantly. You can enhance your performance, build stronger professional relationships, and succeed in various non-sales roles by leveraging your communication abilities, relationship-building skills, persuasive capabilities, customer focus, goal orientation, problem-solving aptitude, adaptability, and data analysis expertise. Embrace and apply your sales skills strategically, and you will unlock new opportunities for growth and advancement in your chosen career path.

Let's continue exploring the ways your sales skills can benefit your non-sales job:

✓ Presentation Skills: Sales professionals often deliver engaging and persuasive presentations to clients. This experience translates well into non-sales roles where presentations are integral to sharing information, pitching ideas, or delivering project updates. Your sales skills can help you structure your presentations effectively, engage your audience, and deliver compelling messages that resonate and leave a lasting impact.

✓ Customer Service Excellence: Sales professionals understand the importance of exceptional customer service. This customer-centric mindset can be applied in non-sales jobs where internal or external customers play a significant role. By employing your sales skills, you can deliver personalized service, anticipate customer needs, and go above and beyond to exceed their expectations. Your commitment to customer satisfaction will build strong relationships and foster a positive work environment.

✓ Time Management: Sales professionals must juggle multiple tasks, prioritize activities, and manage their time efficiently to meet targets. This time management expertise is highly valuable in non-sales roles where workload and deadlines are common challenges. By leveraging your sales skills, you can effectively plan your work, set priorities, and allocate your time wisely. This ensures you meet deadlines, maintain productivity, and achieve optimal results in your non-sales job.

✓ Market Awareness: Sales professionals continuously stay informed about market trends, competitor activities, and industry developments. This market awareness can be advantageous in non-sales roles that require a deep understanding of the industry landscape. By leveraging your sales experience, you can contribute valuable insights, identify emerging opportunities, and adapt strategies to stay competitive. Your market awareness adds depth to your decision-making and positions you as a valuable asset in your non-sales role.

Incorporating these sales skills into your non-sales job can significantly enhance your performance, contribute to your professional growth, and open up new opportunities. Embrace the transferability of your sales skills and apply them strategically in your non-sales role. By doing so, you will maximize your potential, stand out among your peers, and achieve success beyond the boundaries of traditional sales roles.

# Chapter 7: Unlocking Career Advancement with Sales Techniques

Sales techniques are not limited to the realm of sales. They can be powerful tools for unlocking career advancement and success in various professional fields. Adopting and applying key sales techniques can enhance your professional effectiveness, build strong relationships, and propel your career forward. Let's explore how you can leverage sales techniques to unlock career advancement. Effective networking is one of the fundamental sales techniques that can benefit your career advancement.

Networking is a powerful tool for establishing connections, expanding your professional circle, and creating opportunities. You can approach networking with a strategic mindset by utilizing your sales skills. This involves identifying key individuals in your industry, attending relevant events, and actively engaging in conversations. Building authentic relationships allows you to tap into new opportunities, gain valuable insights, and increase visibility within your professional community.

Another crucial sales technique for career advancement is the ability to articulate and communicate your value proposition. Sales professionals are skilled at clearly and compellingly presenting the value of their products or services to potential customers. In your career, you must effectively communicate your unique skills, experiences, and contributions to employers or decision-makers. By showcasing your value proposition, you can position yourself as a valuable asset and increase your chances of career advancement.

Sales professionals also understand the importance of continuous learning and self-improvement. To advance your career, it is crucial to stay updated with industry trends, develop new skills, and seek opportunities for professional development. By adopting a sales mindset, you can actively pursue learning opportunities, attend relevant workshops or seminars, and stay ahead of the curve in your field. This commitment to self-improvement demonstrates your dedication to growth and positions you as a proactive and valuable professional. Building and maintaining strong relationships is another key sales aspect that can unlock career advancement. Sales professionals excel at building rapport and trust with their clients.

By leveraging your sales techniques, such as active listening, empathy, and effective communication, you can build mutually beneficial relationships that open doors to new opportunities, mentorship, and career advancement. Sales techniques also emphasize the importance of setting and achieving goals. Successful sales professionals are accustomed to setting ambitious targets and developing strategies. By utilizing sales techniques like goal setting, time management, and tracking progress, you can maintain focus, measure your success, and make informed decisions to advance your career. The art of persuasion is another critical sales technique that can benefit your career advancement. Sales professionals are skilled at influencing and persuading others to take desired actions. In your career, the ability to persuade and influence decision-makers, colleagues, or clients can significantly impact your advancement opportunities.

By employing sales techniques such as effective communication, presenting compelling arguments, and addressing objections, you can position yourself as a persuasive and influential professional who can drive positive change and achieve desired outcomes. Sales professionals are also adept at adapting to change and overcoming obstacles. They are resilient and can navigate through challenges to achieve their sales targets.

These qualities are equally valuable in career advancement. By embracing change, adapting to new technologies or market dynamics, and demonstrating resilience in the face of setbacks, you can showcase your ability to thrive in dynamic environments. This adaptability and resilience can position you as a valuable asset and increase your chances of career advancement.

In addition to these techniques, sales professionals understand the importance of a positive mindset and a results-oriented approach. A positive mindset fuels motivation, creativity, and resilience, while a results-oriented approach drives productivity and achievement. By adopting these attitudes and applying them to your career, you can overcome obstacles, maintain focus on your goals, and consistently deliver outstanding results. This mindset differentiates high-performing professionals and increases your chances of career advancement.

There are some additional ways in which sales techniques can unlock career advancement:

✓ Problem-Solving Skills: Sales professionals often encounter complex challenges and are skilled at finding creative solutions. This problem-solving ability can be applied to various career situations. By utilizing your sales techniques, such as analyzing situations, identifying needs, and proposing solutions, you can showcase your problem-solving skills to employers or decision-makers. This demonstrates your ability to tackle complex problems, think critically, and contribute to the advancement of your organization.

✓   Customer Focus: Sales professionals prioritize the needs and preferences of their customers. By utilizing your sales techniques, such as active listening and gathering feedback, you can identify opportunities for improvement and deliver solutions that align with the needs of your "customers." This customer-centric approach enhances your professional reputation and contributes to career advancement.

✓   Data Analysis: Sales professionals use data analysis to identify trends, make informed decisions, and optimize strategies. This analytical skill set is highly valuable in non-sales roles where data-driven decision-making is crucial. By applying your sales techniques, such as data collection, analysis, and interpretation, you can contribute valuable insights to your organization. Your ability to make data-informed recommendations or drive data-driven initiatives positions you as a valuable asset and supports your career advancement.

✓    Leadership Abilities: Sales professionals often work autonomously and possess strong leadership qualities. These leadership abilities can be transferred to non-sales roles, allowing you to take on leadership responsibilities and drive initiatives. By leveraging your sales techniques, such as self-motivation, goal orientation, and the ability to influence and inspire others, you can emerge as a natural leader within your organization. This leadership potential enhances your professional profile and opens doors for career advancement opportunities.

✓    Presentation and Communication: Sales professionals deliver impactful presentations and communicate effectively with clients. These presentation and communication skills are highly transferable to non-sales roles where effective communication is key. By utilizing your sales techniques, such as crafting compelling messages, delivering engaging presentations, and tailoring your communication style to different audiences, you can effectively convey information, influence stakeholders, and gain recognition for your excellent communication skills. This enhances your professional reputation and contributes to career advancement.

✓ Customer-Centric Problem Solving: Sales professionals address customer pain points and provide solutions. This customer-centric problem-solving approach can be applied in non-sales roles as well. By utilizing your sales techniques, such as understanding user needs, analyzing challenges, and proposing effective solutions, you can contribute to problem-solving initiatives within your organization. Your ability to think from the perspective of different stakeholders and propose customer-centric solutions sets you apart and accelerates your career advancement.

Applying sales techniques extends beyond the sales domain and can significantly contribute to career advancement in various professional fields. Leveraging your skills can unlock new opportunities and accelerate your career growth.

# Chapter 8: Balancing Sales Demands with Your Professional Life

Achieving a work-life balance is a universal challenge, but it can be particularly demanding for individuals in sales roles. Sales professionals often face pressure to meet targets, manage client relationships, and maintain high productivity. However, balancing professional responsibilities and personal well-being is crucial to avoid burnout and foster a fulfilling life. This means defining specific working hours and committing to respecting personal time outside of those hours.

By setting boundaries, you create space for relaxation, hobbies, family time, and self-care, all vital for your overall well-being. Effective time management is another important aspect of balancing sales demands with your professional life. Sales professionals often have numerous tasks to handle simultaneously, such as prospecting, meetings, and administrative work.

By prioritizing tasks and utilizing time management techniques, such as creating to-do lists, using productivity tools, and allocating specific time slots for different activities. In addition to time management, delegation can be a valuable strategy for balancing sales demands. Recognize that you cannot handle everything independently and that delegating tasks to capable team members or leveraging support resources can lighten your workload.

Delegation allows you to focus on high-value activities while ensuring that other essential tasks are efficiently handled. This reduces stress and creates opportunities for growth and development within your team. Maintaining open communication is another critical factor in achieving work-life balance in sales.

Communicating your needs and limitations to your superiors, colleagues, and clients is essential. By clearly expressing your availability, setting realistic expectations, and negotiating deadlines or commitments, you can manage the demands of your professional life without sacrificing your well-being. Open communication fosters understanding and collaboration, enabling a healthier balance between work and personal life.

In the pursuit of work-life balance, it is crucial to prioritize self-care. Incorporate activities that promote self-care into your routine, such as exercise, meditation, hobbies, spending time with loved ones, or pursuing personal interests. These activities rejuvenate you and enhance your overall performance and job satisfaction. While it provides flexibility and connectivity, it can also blur the boundaries between work and personal life.

It is crucial to establish healthy technology habits by setting designated periods for disconnecting, such as turning off work notifications during personal time. Creating technology boundaries ensures you can fully engage with your personal life without constant work interruptions. Flexibility is another key aspect of achieving work-life balance in sales.

Take advantage of flexible work arrangements, such as remote work or flexible schedules, whenever possible. Flexibility allows you to accommodate personal commitments and responsibilities, giving you the freedom to manage both your professional and personal life effectively. Seeking support from your organization or seeking external resources can greatly assist in balancing sales demands with your professional life.

Many companies offer employee assistance programs, wellness, and work-life balance initiatives. Take advantage of these resources for guidance, support, and tools to achieve a healthy balance. Additionally, connecting with professional networks or seeking guidance from mentors in the sales field can provide valuable insights and strategies for managing the demands of a sales career while maintaining personal well-being. Achieving work-life balance in sales requires a proactive approach and a commitment to self-care.

By setting boundaries, effectively managing your time, delegating tasks, maintaining open communication, prioritizing self-care, establishing healthy technology habits, embracing flexibility, and seeking support, you can create a harmonious integration of your sales career and personal life. Balancing sales demands with your professional life promotes your well-being and enhances your effectiveness as a sales professional, allowing you to thrive personally and professionally.

It is important to cultivate a mindset emphasizing work-life integration rather than strict separation. Instead of viewing work and personal life as separate entities, consider how they can complement and support each other. For example, the skills and strategies you develop in sales, such as effective communication and negotiation, can benefit your relationships and interactions outside work. Likewise, the fulfilment and satisfaction you derive from your personal life can positively impact your performance and motivation in your sales career. When striving for work-life balance in sales, it is also crucial to establish clear priorities. Reflect on your values and what truly matters to you. Identify your long-term goals and aspirations in your career and personal life.

By aligning your actions and decisions with your priorities, you can make intentional choices that promote a healthier balance and prevent feeling overwhelmed or stretched too thin. Another aspect to consider is the importance of self-reflection and self-awareness. Assess your energy levels, emotional well-being, and overall satisfaction with your current work-life balance. Regularly check in with yourself and make adjustments as needed. This self-awareness allows you to proactively address any imbalances or areas of dissatisfaction, ensuring that you can make conscious choices to create a more fulfilling and harmonious work-life blend.

In addition, learning to manage stress effectively is crucial in balancing sales demands with your personal life. Sales can be a high-pressure environment, and developing healthy coping mechanisms to navigate stress is essential. Explore stress management techniques that work for you, such as mindfulness meditation, exercise, journaling, or engaging in hobbies that help you relax and recharge.

You can prevent burnout and maintain a sustainable work-life balance by managing stress proactively. A supportive network is invaluable when it comes to work-life balance in sales. Surround yourself with individuals who understand your profession's challenges and demands and support your efforts to achieve balance. Seek mentors or colleagues who have successfully navigated the delicate balance between work and personal life and learn from their experiences. Engage in open and honest conversations with your support network, sharing your struggles and seeking advice and encouragement.

Embrace the concept of self-care as a non-negotiable aspect of work-life balance. Self-care encompasses various dimensions, including physical, emotional, and mental well-being. Prioritize activities that nourish and rejuvenate you, such as regular exercise, quality sleep, healthy eating and practicing self-compassion. By investing in self-care, you recharge your energy, enhance your resilience, and ensure you can meet the demands of your sales career and personal life. Achieving work-life balance in sales requires a mindful and intentional approach.

By cultivating a mindset of integration, establishing clear priorities, practicing self-reflection and self-awareness, managing stress effectively, adopting boundary management strategies, building a supportive network, and prioritizing self-care, you can create a sustainable and fulfilling balance between your sales career and personal life. Remember, work-life balance is a continuous journey requiring effort and adjustments. Dedication and a proactive mindset can create a harmonious blend that promotes professional success and personal well-being.

# Chapter 9: The Art of Persuasion in Your Personal Life

Persuasion is a powerful skill that extends beyond the realm of sales and can significantly impact your personal life. Whether trying to influence a family member, negotiate with a friend, or convince someone to see things from your perspective, mastering the art of persuasion can enhance your relationships and help you achieve your personal goals. In this chapter, we will explore the principles and techniques of persuasion that can be applied in various aspects of your life.

Effective persuasion begins with understanding the needs, desires, and motivations of the person you are trying to influence. Take the time to listen actively and empathetically, putting yourself in their shoes to gain insight into their perspective. By demonstrating genuine interest and understanding, you can establish trust and rapport, creating a conducive environment for persuasion. One essential aspect of persuasion is communicating your ideas clearly and compellingly.

Craft your message to resonate with the other person's values and priorities. Tailor your language and approach to their communication style, ensuring your message is easily understood and relatable.

People are more likely to be persuaded by individuals they trust and respect. Establish your credibility by showcasing your expertise, sharing relevant experiences or success stories, or leveraging the opinions and endorsements of others. By positioning yourself as knowledgeable and trustworthy, you increase the likelihood of accepting your ideas. Emotional appeal is another powerful tool in persuasion.

Humans are driven by emotions, and tapping into those emotions can help you make a compelling case. Appeal to the values, desires, and emotions of the person you are trying to persuade. Show how your proposal aligns with their aspirations, addresses their concerns, solves their problems, or can bring about positive emotions such as joy, security, or belonging. The social proof involves highlighting the experiences or opinions of others who have already embraced your proposal or perspective.

It creates a sense of belonging and the perception that many others have made a similar choice, making it more likely for the person to follow suit. Scarcity emphasizes your proposal's limited availability or time sensitivity, creating a sense of urgency and the fear of missing out. Active listening plays a crucial role in persuasive communication.

By attentively listening to the other person's concerns, objections, and feedback, you can address their points and adapt your approach accordingly. Demonstrate empathy, validate their feelings, and show that you genuinely value their input. This enhances your understanding of their perspective and fosters a collaborative atmosphere where mutually beneficial solutions can be reached. Flexibility and adaptability are essential for persuasion in your personal life.

Recognize that different people respond to different approaches; what works in one situation may not work in another. Be open to adjusting your strategies, revising your proposals, or exploring alternative options that accommodate the needs and preferences of the person you are trying to persuade. Demonstrating flexibility shows that you are genuinely interested in finding common ground and reaching a mutually satisfying outcome.

It is important to note that persuasion should always be approached ethically and with respect for the autonomy and free will of others. The goal is not to manipulate or coerce but to present compelling arguments and ideas. Respecting boundaries, acknowledging diverse perspectives, and being open to different outcomes are fundamental principles of ethical persuasion.

A few more strategies can enhance your persuasive abilities in your personal life. One such strategy is the power of storytelling. Humans are wired to connect with stories, which can be a compelling way to convey your message and make it memorable.

Craft narratives that illustrate your points share personal experiences, or use relatable anecdotes to engage the emotions and imagination of the person you are trying to persuade. Another important aspect of persuasion is the ability to find common ground, and highlight shared interests. By focusing on mutual benefits and emphasizing how your proposal aligns with the goals and aspirations of the other person, you create a sense of collaboration and increase the likelihood of them being open to your ideas.

Show them that your proposal is not solely self-serving but a win-win situation that can lead to positive outcomes for both parties. Building rapport and fostering positive relationships are foundational elements of effective persuasion. People are more likely to be receptive to your ideas if they genuinely connect with you. Show genuine interest in the other person's well-being, actively engage in meaningful conversations, and support their goals and aspirations.

When people feel valued and understood, they are more likely to be open to your influence. It is also important to be mindful of your non-verbal communication. Maintain an open and confident body posture, make eye contact, and use a warm and friendly tone. Non-verbal cues can convey sincerity, authenticity, and trustworthiness, enhancing your persuasive efforts. Timing is another crucial factor in persuasive communication. Choose the right moment to present your ideas, considering the person's emotional state, availability, and receptiveness. It is often more effective to approach someone when they are relaxed and receptive rather than stressed or preoccupied.

By choosing the opportune moment, you increase the chances of your message being well-received. It is important to be patient and resilient in your pursuit of persuasion. Not everyone may be immediately convinced or open to your ideas. People have their own beliefs, biases, and preferences, which may require time and consistent effort to influence.

Be prepared for setbacks and objections, and approach them with a positive and solution-oriented mindset.

Adapt your approach, address concerns, and be persistent while respecting the other person's autonomy. The art of persuasion extends beyond sales and can greatly impact your personal life. You can enhance your persuasive abilities in various personal situations by utilizing strategies such as storytelling, finding common ground, building rapport, leveraging non-verbal communication, choosing the right timing, and being patient and resilient.

Remember to approach persuasion ethically and with respect for others' autonomy. With practice and a genuine desire to create positive outcomes, you can become a more effective and influential communicator in your personal life.

# Chapter 10: How Sales Skills Can Improve Your Finances

Sales skills are not limited to the realm of business and can have a significant impact on your finances. By applying the principles and techniques of sales to your financial decisions and practices, you can enhance your earning potential, make better financial choices, and ultimately achieve greater financial success.

This chapter will explore how sales skills can improve your finances and set you toward financial well-being. One of the key aspects of sales is the ability to identify and seize opportunities. This mindset can be directly applied to your finances. By being proactive and vigilant, you can spot opportunities to increase your income or save money. Find additional income through freelance work, side gigs, or entrepreneurial ventures. Explore investment opportunities that align with your financial goals and risk tolerance. By having a sales-oriented mindset, you become more attuned to financial opportunities and are better positioned to capitalize on them.

Effective salespeople understand the importance of building relationships with their customers. This principle holds when it comes to personal finances as well. Cultivating strong relationships with financial advisors, bankers, and industry professionals can provide valuable insights, guidance, and access to opportunities. These relationships can help you make informed decisions, optimize your financial strategies, and stay abreast of market trends and investment options. Sales skills also involve effective communication and negotiation. These skills can be instrumental in managing your finances.

When dealing with financial institutions or service providers, such as banks, insurance companies, or credit card companies, effective communication and negotiation can help you secure better terms, lower fees, or favorable interest rates. Sales professionals are skilled at managing objections and overcoming resistance. These skills can be applied to personal finance by addressing common roadblocks and challenges that hinder financial success. For example, suppose you struggle with controlling impulsive spending. Applying sales techniques such as highlighting the long-term benefits of saving or using visualization techniques to reinforce your financial goals can help you overcome impulsive buying behaviors.

You can develop strategies to navigate your financial obstacles effectively by identifying and addressing them. Salespeople understand the importance of persistence and resilience. These qualities are equally valuable in personal finance. Building wealth and achieving financial goals often require long-term commitment and perseverance. Sales skills can help you stay focused on your financial objectives, despite setbacks or challenges.

By maintaining a positive mindset, adapting to changing circumstances, and continuously seeking opportunities to improve your financial situation, you increase your chances of long-term financial success. The ability to influence and persuade is another key aspect of sales skills. In personal finance, being persuasive can help you secure better deals, negotiate favorable terms, or convince others to support your financial goals.

Whether it's persuading your partner to adhere to a budget, negotiating with creditors for lower interest rates, or convincing family members to embrace frugal habits, the art of persuasion can positively impact your finances. Sales professionals often excel at time management and prioritization. These skills are equally important when it comes to personal finance. Managing time effectively lets you focus on income-generating activities, budgeting, and financial planning. By setting clear financial goals, prioritizing your spending and saving, and allocating your resources wisely, you can optimize your financial situation and progress towards your long-term objectives. Sales professionals understand the importance of setting and achieving goals.

They create clear objectives and develop actionable plans to reach them. This goal-oriented approach can be directly applied to personal finance. This sales-inspired goal-setting methodology can help you stay focused and motivated in achieving your financial objectives. Effective salespeople are skilled at managing objections and addressing customer concerns. This skill is valuable when it comes to personal finance as well. Financial decisions often involve weighing options, assessing risks, and addressing potential obstacles.

By adopting a sales mindset, you can approach financial decisions with a critical eye, identify potential objections or challenges, and develop strategies to overcome them. This proactive approach lets you make well-informed choices and minimize potential financial setbacks. Sales professionals understand the importance of building a strong personal brand and reputation. In personal finance, your reputation and creditworthiness play a crucial role. Lenders, landlords, and financial institutions rely on your credit history and reputation to assess your financial trustworthiness.

By managing your finances responsibly, paying bills on time, and maintaining a good credit score, you enhance your financial reputation and gain access to better financial opportunities. Just like a salesperson aims to build trust with their customers, you can build trust with financial institutions by demonstrating responsible financial behavior. Negotiation skills are a fundamental aspect of sales, and they can be applied to personal finance to your advantage. Whether negotiating a better interest rate on loan, haggling for a lower price on a major purchase, or bargaining for a salary increase, having strong negotiation skills can save you money and improve your financial standing.

By researching market prices, preparing persuasive arguments, and effectively communicating your needs and interests, you can negotiate more favorable terms that benefit your financial situation. Sales professionals understand the importance of continuous learning and self-improvement. In the ever-evolving world of sales, staying updated on industry trends, market changes, and new techniques is essential for success.

The same principle applies to personal finance. By staying informed about personal finance topics and staying abreast of changes in tax laws, investment opportunities, and financial strategies, you can make more informed decisions and adapt your financial plans accordingly. Continuously educate yourself on personal finance through books, online resources, and financial literacy programs to enhance your financial knowledge and make sound financial choices.

Furthermore, sales skills emphasize the importance of building and maintaining relationships. This principle is equally applicable to personal finance. Networking and fostering relationships with professionals in the finance industry, such as financial advisors, can provide valuable insights and guidance on managing your finances. Building a network of trusted individuals who can offer financial advice and share their expertise can significantly benefit your financial journey.

Sales professionals understand resilience's significance in facing rejection and setbacks. Financial challenges and unexpected expenses are common, and the ability to bounce back and adapt is crucial. Adopting a resilient mindset allows you to view setbacks as learning opportunities, make necessary adjustments, and persevere in achieving your financial goals.

This resilience helps you maintain a positive outlook and find creative solutions to overcome obstacles, ultimately leading to long-term financial stability. Sales skills have a direct impact on personal finances. You can enhance your financial well-being by setting goals, managing objections, building a strong personal brand, utilizing negotiation skills, embracing continuous learning, fostering relationships, and cultivating resilience.

Applying these sales principles to your personal finance journey will enable you to make informed decisions. Embracing sales skills can empower you to control your finances and build a secure and prosperous future.

# Chapter 11: Sales Techniques for a Successful Job Search

Incorporating sales techniques can significantly enhance your chances of success when searching for a job. Just as sales professionals use various strategies to close deals and win customers, you can apply similar principles to stand out in the competitive job market and secure the job of your dreams. Effective communication is one of the key sales techniques that can be applied to a job search. In sales, communication is vital for building relationships and understanding customer needs.

Similarly, effective communication lets you convey your skills, qualifications, and enthusiasm to potential employers during a job search. Crafting a compelling resume and cover letter highlighting your relevant experience, achievements, and strengths. Tailor your communication to each job application, showcasing how your skills align with the role's requirements.

During interviews, focus on articulating your value proposition and demonstrating your passion for the position. Clear and persuasive communication will set you apart from other candidates and leave a lasting impression on hiring managers. Another important sales technique for a successful job search is conducting thorough research. Sales professionals extensively research their target audience to understand their needs and preferences.

It would help to research the companies you're interested in working for. Gain insights into their mission, values, culture, products or services, and recent achievements. This knowledge will help you customize your application materials and enable you to ask informed questions during interviews, showcasing your genuine interest and enthusiasm.

Researching the industry trends and developments will also equip you with valuable information to discuss during interviews, demonstrating your knowledge and commitment. As salespeople build and expand their networks, networking is crucial in a job search.

Connect with professionals in your desired industry through platforms like LinkedIn, attend industry events, and join relevant professional associations. Networking can lead to valuable connections, referrals, and hidden job opportunities. Engage in conversations, build relationships, and seek advice from experienced professionals.

Effective networking allows you to tap into the hidden job market, where many positions are filled through word-of-mouth referrals before they are advertised. You may become the top candidate for an unadvertised opportunity by nurturing relationships and showcasing your skills. Sales professionals excel at showcasing their value and differentiating themselves from competitors. Developing a personal brand that highlights your unique qualities and skills is essential in a job search.

Determine your unique selling points (USPs) and create a strong personal brand that aligns with the needs and values of your target employers. This could involve showcasing specific expertise, industry certifications, or notable achievements. Establish an online presence by maintaining a professional online profile.

By effectively differentiating yourself, you will capture the attention of hiring managers and leave a memorable impression. In sales, persistence and follow-up are crucial to closing deals. After submitting your application, follow up with a personalized thank-you note or email to express your appreciation and reiterate your interest in the position. If you don't hear back within a reasonable timeframe, don't hesitate to follow up to inquire about the status of your application. Persistence shows your enthusiasm and commitment to the opportunity. However, it's important to strike a balance and avoid being overly persistent, as it may come across as pushy or desperate. Sales professionals are skilled at handling objections and overcoming barriers.

In a job search, you may encounter objections or concerns from potential employers. These objections could be related to gaps in your employment history, lack of specific experience, or a career change.

Anticipate and proactively address these objections in your application materials or during interviews. Highlight transferable skills, relevant projects or volunteer work, and demonstrate your ability to adapt and learn quickly. Addressing objections, head-on can alleviate potential concerns and showcase your suitability for the role.

In addition to the sales mentioned above techniques, relationship building is another valuable skill that can contribute to a successful job search. Sales professionals understand the importance of building strong client relationships to foster trust and loyalty. Similarly, building relationships with key individuals in a job search can open doors to new opportunities. Attend industry events, job fairs, and networking functions to meet professionals from various organizations.

Engage in meaningful conversations, show genuine interest in others, and seek opportunities to add value. Building relationships can lead to valuable connections, insider information about job openings, and recommendations from influential individuals within the industry. Sales professionals also know the significance of understanding customer needs and tailoring their approach accordingly. This customer-centric mindset can be applied to a job search by tailoring your application materials and interviews to align with the needs and goals of the hiring organization.

Take the time to analyze the job description and understand the requirements and qualifications they seek. During interviews, emphasize how your expertise and abilities can contribute to the organization's success and solve its challenges. Adaptability is another valuable sales skill that can benefit your job search. Sales professionals often face unexpected challenges, changing market conditions, and evolving customer demands. They must adapt their strategies and approaches to stay competitive and meet their targets.

Adapting and pivoting are crucial in a job search. The job market is constantly changing, and new trends and technologies emerge. It's essential to stay updated on industry developments, acquire new skills if necessary, and be open to different opportunities that may align with your interests and capabilities. Demonstrating your adaptability and willingness to learn and grow will make you an attractive candidate to potential employers. Sales professionals are also skilled in managing objections and handling rejection.

You may inevitably face rejection or encounter employer objections in a job search. It's important not to let these setbacks discourage you. Instead, view them as learning opportunities and stepping stones toward success. Analyze the feedback you receive, identify areas for improvement, and make necessary adjustments to your approach. Maintain a positive mindset, stay resilient, and continue to refine your skills and strategies. You will become a stronger and more competitive candidate in the job market by approaching rejection as a chance to grow and improve.

Incorporating sales techniques into your job search can be highly beneficial. Building relationships, tailoring your approach to meet the employer's needs, embracing adaptability, managing objections and rejection, and demonstrating persistence and follow-up are all valuable skills and strategies employed by successful sales professionals.

Adopting these techniques allows you to differentiate yourself and secure your desired job. So, apply sales principles to your job search and pave the way for a successful career transition.

# Chapter 12: The Importance of Sales Skills in Entrepreneurship

Entrepreneurship is a dynamic and challenging journey requiring diverse skills to navigate the ever-changing business landscape. While many may associate sales skills solely with traditional sales roles, the truth is that these skills are also invaluable for entrepreneurs. In this chapter, we delve into the importance of sales skills in entrepreneurship and explore how they can contribute to the success of your venture.

One of the key reasons why sales skills are vital for entrepreneurs is that they enable you to effectively communicate the value of your product or service to potential customers. As an entrepreneur, you must convince others that your offering is worth their time, attention, and financial investment.

This involves crafting a compelling sales pitch highlighting your product or service's unique features, benefits, and competitive advantages. By leveraging your sales skills, you can persuasively articulate the value proposition, addressing your target audience's pain points and needs. This ability to communicate persuasively is crucial for attracting customers and generating sales. Sales skills play a significant role in building and nurturing relationships with customers.

Successful entrepreneurs understand the importance of developing long-term, mutually beneficial relationships with their customer base. Entrepreneurs can deeply understand their customers' needs and preferences by employing effective sales techniques such as active listening, empathy, and relationship building. This understanding allows them to tailor their offerings, provide personalized solutions, and ultimately cultivate customer loyalty and repeat business.

Sales skills also enable entrepreneurs to effectively handle objections and address any concerns or doubts that potential customers may have, fostering trust and credibility. Sales skills are also crucial for forging partnerships and collaborations. As an entrepreneur, you may need to negotiate deals with suppliers, distributors, investors, or other business partners.

The ability to negotiate effectively and create mutually beneficial agreements is instrumental in establishing strategic alliances and securing favorable terms. Sales skills such as persuasive communication, problem-solving, and the art of negotiation can help you navigate these discussions and reach agreements that support the growth and success of your business.

Another aspect where sales skills come into play in entrepreneurship is the identification and acquisition of new customers. Entrepreneurs constantly seek opportunities to expand their customer base and reach new markets. This requires proactive prospecting, lead generation, and effective sales strategies.

Sales skills enable entrepreneurs to identify potential customers, engage them in meaningful conversations, and convert them into paying clients. By leveraging your sales skills, you can effectively pitch your product or service, address objections, and close deals. This ability to acquire new customers is vital for the growth and sustainability of your business. Sales skills can also contribute to the development of effective marketing strategies.

Entrepreneurs must understand their target market, identify unique selling propositions, and create compelling marketing messages. Sales skills provide insights into customer behavior, market trends, and competitive dynamics. This understanding allows you to develop targeted marketing campaigns, craft persuasive sales materials, and effectively position your brand in the marketplace.

Applying your sales skills to marketing can attract the right audience, differentiate yourself from competitors, and ultimately drive business growth. Sales skills are closely tied to the ability to adapt and pivot in response to market changes. Entrepreneurs operate in a dynamic environment where customer needs, preferences, and market conditions can evolve rapidly.

Sales professionals are accustomed to navigating changing landscapes and adjusting their strategies accordingly. By embracing a sales mindset, entrepreneurs can stay agile, identify new opportunities, and pivot their business models or offerings when necessary. This flexibility and adaptability are essential for staying competitive and sustaining long-term success in the entrepreneurial journey.

Additionally, sales skills give entrepreneurs the confidence and resilience to overcome challenges and setbacks. As an entrepreneur, you will inevitably face rejections, objections, and obstacles along your journey. Sales professionals are trained to handle rejection gracefully and view it as an opportunity for growth. They understand that every "no" brings them one step closer to a "yes."

By adopting a sales mindset, entrepreneurs can develop a resilient attitude and embrace failure as a stepping stone to success. They can learn from their experiences, refine their approaches, and persistently pursue their goals. Sales skills empower entrepreneurs to become effective leaders within their organizations. Whether you have a small team or are leading a larger workforce, the ability to inspire and motivate others is crucial. Sales professionals are skilled at influencing and inspiring action within their sales teams and with their customers.

By applying sales principles to leadership, entrepreneurs can create high-performing teams, drive collaboration, and foster a positive and productive work environment. Sales skills equip entrepreneurs to gather and analyze valuable market intelligence. Understanding market trends, customer preferences, and competitive dynamics is essential for making informed business decisions. Sales professionals are trained to gather insights through customer interactions, competitor analysis, and market research.

By applying these skills to entrepreneurship, you can identify emerging opportunities, assess the viability of new business ideas, and make data-driven decisions that give your venture a competitive edge. Sales skills also contribute to effective time management and prioritization. Entrepreneurs often face competing demands and limited resources.

By adopting sales techniques such as pipeline management, prospect prioritization, and efficient communication, you can optimize your time and focus on activities that drive revenue and business growth. Sales skills help you identify high-value prospects, nurture relationships with key stakeholders, and allocate your time and energy to activities that impact your business's success.

The importance of sales skills in entrepreneurship cannot be overstated. From effective communication and relationship building to negotiation, marketing, leadership, and strategic decision-making, sales skills provide entrepreneurs a versatile toolkit for success.

By embracing and honing these skills, entrepreneurs can enhance their ability to attract customers, drive revenue, adapt to market changes, and build a thriving and sustainable business.

So, leverage the power of sales skills in your entrepreneurial endeavors and unlock your full potential for success.

# Chapter 13: The Role of Empathy in Both Sales and Personal Relationships

Empathy plays a vital role in sales and personal relationships, allowing individuals to connect on a deeper level, understand others' perspectives, and build meaningful connections. In Chapter 13, we explore the significance of empathy in these contexts and how it influences our interactions and outcomes. When sales professionals demonstrate empathy, they genuinely care and understand customers' needs and concerns. By actively listening and putting themselves in the customers' shoes, salespeople can better comprehend their challenges, desires, and motivations. This understanding enables them to offer personalized solutions that resonate with customers, increasing customer satisfaction and sales.

Empathy in sales goes beyond merely understanding customers' surface-level needs. It involves recognizing and addressing their underlying emotions, fears, and aspirations. Sales professionals who can tap into customers' emotions and provide reassurance or relief are likelier to establish a strong emotional connection. This emotional connection fosters trust, loyalty, and long-term customer relationships, ultimately benefiting the salesperson and the customer. Beyond the sales context, empathy is equally essential in personal relationships. When we empathize with others, we demonstrate our capacity to care for and support them genuinely. Empathy allows us to step outside our perspective and experience the world through the eyes of our loved ones, friends, or colleagues. It helps us understand their joys, struggles, and challenges, fostering deeper connections and enhancing the quality of our relationships.

Empathy helps create an environment of open communication and mutual understanding in personal relationships. When we empathize with others, we validate their emotions and experiences, showing them that we value and respect their feelings. This validation builds trust and encourages individuals to share more openly, leading to healthier and more fulfilling relationships. Empathy also plays a crucial role in conflict resolution and problem-solving within personal relationships.

By empathizing with the perspectives of others involved in a conflict, we can better comprehend their motivations and concerns. This understanding enables us to find common ground, seek compromises, and work towards mutually beneficial solutions. Through empathy, we create a safe space for open dialogue, fostering collaboration and harmony. Empathy strengthens our ability to provide emotional support to those around us. We can offer comfort, encouragement, and a listening ear by empathizing with others during challenging times.

Empathy allows us to be present and attuned to the needs of others, providing them with the validation and understanding they seek. This support strengthens our relationships and helps create a sense of belonging and connectedness. It is worth noting that empathy is not limited to understanding and supporting others during difficult times. It also encompasses celebrating their successes and joys. By empathizing with others' happiness and sharing their joy, we deepen our emotional connection and foster a positive and uplifting environment in our relationships. Empathy also promotes effective communication in both sales and personal relationships.

When we empathize with others, we listen to their words and tune in to their non-verbal cues, emotions, and subtle nuances. This deep level of understanding allows us to respond in a way that addresses their needs and concerns effectively. In sales, empathetic communication helps salespeople ask the right questions, provide relevant information, and tailor their approach to suit each customer's unique situation. In personal relationships, empathy allows us to be more attentive listeners, validating the experiences of others and responding with empathy and compassion.

In addition to communication, empathy cultivates a sense of compassion and kindness. When we empathize with others, we develop a genuine concern for their well-being. This compassion extends beyond our needs and desires, allowing us to act selflessly and supportively. In sales, empathetic salespeople go the extra mile to ensure customer satisfaction, providing exceptional service and promptly addressing concerns.

In personal relationships, empathy drives us to offer support, lend a helping hand, or be there for our loved ones during difficult times. This compassion strengthens the bond we share with others and fosters a sense of unity and care. Empathy enhances our ability to navigate differences and conflicts in sales and personal relationships.

We can better understand their perspectives by empathizing with others, even if they differ. This understanding promotes tolerance, respect, and open-mindedness, enabling us to find common ground and seek mutually beneficial solutions. In sales, empathetic salespeople can address customer objections or disagreements by validating their concerns and finding ways to meet their needs effectively.

Empathy helps us overcome differences, resolve conflicts, and strengthen our connection with others in personal relationships. Empathy contributes to personal growth and self-awareness. When we empathize with others, we gain insights into their experiences, emotions, and perspectives. This expanded understanding not only enriches our relationships but also broadens our worldview. By recognizing and appreciating the diverse range of experiences and emotions, we develop a greater sense of empathy towards humanity as a whole. This self-awareness makes us more conscious of our actions and their impact on others, promoting empathy and compassion. Empathy also plays a vital role in building inclusive and diverse environments.

When we empathize with others, we acknowledge their unique identities, backgrounds, and experiences. This recognition fosters inclusivity, respect, and a sense of belonging. In sales, empathetic sales teams are more attuned to the needs and preferences of diverse customer segments, enabling them to provide tailored solutions that resonate with a wide range of individuals. In personal relationships, empathy allows us to celebrate and embrace the differences that make each person unique, fostering a supportive and inclusive atmosphere.

The role of empathy in both sales and personal relationships is undeniable. It enables us to build trust, establish emotional connections, and communicate effectively. Empathy promotes compassion, kindness, and understanding, strengthening bonds and meaningful interactions. By cultivating empathy within ourselves, we can enhance our sales performance, nurture healthier personal relationships, and contribute to a more empathetic and compassionate world.

# Chapter 14: Relationship-Building Techniques That Work in Sales and Personal Life

Building strong and meaningful relationships is a crucial aspect of both sales and personal life. Chapter 14 delves into effective relationship-building techniques in both realms, exploring how they foster connections, trust, and long-term partnerships. One essential technique for relationship building is active listening.

Active listening involves fully engaging with the person speaking, giving them your undivided attention, and seeking to understand their perspective without judgment or interruption. In sales, active listening allows salespeople to accurately grasp customers' needs, preferences, and pain points.

By listening actively, sales professionals can tailor their offerings to meet customers' requirements, ultimately increasing satisfaction and loyalty. Active listening is equally vital in personal relationships.

When we actively listen to our loved ones, friends, or colleagues, we value their thoughts, feelings, and experiences.

This type of attentive listening helps build trust, enhances communication, and fosters deeper connections. Being fully present and engaged in conversations creates an environment where individuals feel heard, understood, and appreciated.

Another technique for relationship building is effective communication. Clear and open communication is key in both sales and personal life. In sales, effective communication involves conveying information about products or services concisely and compellingly.

It also includes responding to customer inquiries, promptly addressing concerns, and providing transparent and honest information. By establishing open lines of communication, salespeople can build trust and credibility with their customers, laying the foundation for successful relationships.

Effective communication is essential for understanding each other's needs, expressing emotions, and resolving conflicts. By practicing clear and empathetic communication, we can avoid misunderstandings, build stronger bonds, and strengthen our relationships. Sharing thoughts, feelings, and aspirations openly helps create an atmosphere of trust and authenticity.

Building rapport is another technique that applies to both sales and personal relationships. Rapport refers to mutual understanding, connection, and harmony between individuals. In sales, building rapport involves finding common ground with customers, establishing shared interests or experiences, and creating positive and friendly interactions.

Sales professionals who build rapport effectively create a more comfortable buying environment, increasing customer satisfaction and loyalty. Building rapport allows us to connect with others on a deeper level in personal relationships. Finding common interests, engaging in meaningful conversations, and showing genuine interest in the lives of our loved ones foster a sense of closeness and connection.

Building rapport helps create a strong foundation for trust and understanding, leading to long-lasting and fulfilling relationships. Trust is a fundamental element in both sales and personal relationships. In sales, trust is crucial as customers need to feel confident in the reliability and credibility of the products or services they purchase.

Sales professionals who consistently deliver on their promises, provide accurate information, and prioritize customer satisfaction earn the trust of their clients, leading to repeat business and referrals. Trust forms the bedrock of a healthy and fulfilling connection in personal relationships.

Trust is built through honesty, reliability, and mutual respect. When individuals trust each other, they feel safe to be vulnerable, share their thoughts and feelings, and rely on each other for support. Trust allows for deeper emotional intimacy and strengthens the bond between individuals. Building relationships requires patience and a genuine interest in others.

In sales, taking the time to understand customers' needs and preferences, and showing a genuine interest in helping them achieve their goals, builds rapport and trust. Investing time and effort into getting to know the other person, understanding their passions, and supporting their aspirations strengthens the connection and demonstrates care and commitment.

Demonstrating appreciation and gratitude is a powerful technique for building relationships. In sales, expressing gratitude to customers for their business and loyalty goes a long way in fostering a positive and lasting connection. Sales professionals who take the time to show appreciation to their clients create a sense of value and importance, leading to stronger relationships and increased customer loyalty.

Expressing gratitude in personal relationships enhances the bond between individuals. Recognizing and acknowledging the contributions, support, and love we receive from our loved ones strengthens the emotional connection and fosters a sense of gratitude.

Appreciating the presence of others in our lives and expressing gratitude for their support and care enhances the quality of our relationships. Effective relationship-building techniques are invaluable in both sales and personal life.

We can cultivate strong, meaningful, and enduring connections by practicing active listening, effective communication, building rapport, fostering trust, demonstrating patience, and expressing appreciation and gratitude. These techniques lay the foundation for successful sales partnerships and enriching personal relationships, ultimately leading to fulfilment and happiness. Empathy plays a significant role in both sales and personal relationships.

Understanding and empathizing with others' emotions, perspectives, and needs is essential for establishing meaningful connections. In sales, empathetic salespeople can put themselves in their customers' shoes, truly understanding their challenges and desires. This allows them to tailor their approach, offer personalized solutions, and build customer trust.

By showing empathy, we validate the emotions and experiences of our loved ones, demonstrating that we care about their well-being. Empathy fosters compassion, strengthens emotional bonds, and creates a supportive and understanding environment where individuals feel valued and heard. Building relationships also involves effective problem-solving and conflict-resolution skills. Resolving customer concerns, addressing objections, and finding win-win solutions are critical for maintaining positive relationships in sales.

Sales professionals who can navigate challenges with professionalism and empathy can turn potential conflicts into opportunities to strengthen customer relationships. Likewise, in personal relationships, conflict resolution skills are essential for maintaining harmony and resolving disagreements constructively. Listening to each other's perspectives, finding common ground, and working towards mutually beneficial solutions.

A positive mindset and attitude are additional elements of successful relationship building. Maintaining a positive attitude in sales, even in the face of rejection or challenges, helps sales professionals persevere and maintain motivation. A positive mindset also radiates to customers, creating a pleasant, engaging interaction that builds rapport.

Practicing effective networking skills is beneficial in both sales and personal relationships. In sales, networking allows professionals to expand their reach, connect with potential clients, and build a network of contacts that can support their business growth.

By attending industry events, joining professional organizations, and engaging in meaningful conversations, salespeople can establish valuable connections contributing to their success. This chapter explores effective relationship-building techniques in both sales and personal life.

We can establish and nurture strong, meaningful, and fulfilling relationships by practicing empathy, adaptability, effective problem-solving, a positive mindset, and networking skills.

These techniques enhance communication, foster trust, and create a supportive and harmonious environment contributing to professional success and personal happiness.

# Chapter 15: Keeping a Sales Mentality in Personal Relationships

Maintaining a sales mentality in personal relationships involves applying some of the key principles and strategies used in sales to enhance the quality of our interactions and connections with others. While the context may differ, the core principles of building rapport, understanding needs, effective communication, and problem-solving remain relevant. This chapter explores how adopting a sales mentality can contribute to stronger and more fulfilling personal relationships.

Building rapport is important to keeping a sales mentality in personal relationships. In sales, building rapport with customers is crucial for establishing trust and creating a positive connection. The same applies to personal relationships. By actively seeking common ground, showing genuine interest in others, and finding shared experiences or interests, we can establish rapport and build a solid foundation for meaningful connections.

Effective communication plays a vital role in both sales and personal relationships. In sales, skilled communicators listen attentively, ask probing questions, and convey information clearly and compellingly.

These communication skills can be applied to personal relationships as well. By actively listening to our loved ones, expressing ourselves clearly and respectfully, and being attentive to their needs and concerns, we can foster open, honest communication that strengthens the individual bond. Successful professionals strive to understand their customers' needs, desires, and pain points in sales to provide tailored solutions. Problem-solving skills are also valuable in personal relationships. In sales, salespeople often encounter obstacles or objections that require creative problem-solving.

Likewise, personal relationships may face challenges that demand thoughtful solutions. By adopting a proactive and solution-oriented mindset, we can address conflicts, resolve issues, and find mutually beneficial outcomes that contribute to the strength and longevity of our relationships. In addition, maintaining a sales mentality in personal relationships involves practicing patience and empathy. Sales professionals understand that building relationships and closing deals requires time and patience. Personal relationships require patience as individuals navigate their differences, grow together, and support each other through life's ups and downs.

Demonstrating empathy, putting ourselves in others' shoes, and showing understanding and compassion contribute to nurturing and sustaining healthy and harmonious personal relationships. A sales mentality also involves setting goals and measuring progress. In sales, professionals set targets, track their progress, and adjust as needed to achieve their objectives.

Applying this mindset to personal relationships can help individuals identify areas for improvement, set goals for personal growth, and measure their progress in building stronger connections with their loved ones. By continuously striving to deepen the bond and enhance the quality of the relationship, individuals can create a more fulfilling and rewarding personal life.

A sales mentality encourages individuals to take ownership of their actions and responsibilities. In sales, professionals understand the importance of accountability and taking the initiative to deliver results. Similarly, in personal relationships, taking responsibility for our actions, acknowledging our mistakes, and actively working towards resolving conflicts or improving ourselves contributes to healthier and more satisfying relationships. A sales mentality encourages individuals to embrace a growth mindset. In sales, professionals constantly seek ways to improve their skills, learn from their experiences, and adapt to changing circumstances.

Adopting a growth mindset in personal relationships means being open to learning and growth, recognizing that relationships evolve, and being willing to adapt to the changing dynamics and needs of our loved ones. Keeping a sales mentality in personal relationships involves being proactive and proactive. In sales, professionals take the initiative by reaching out to potential customers, following up on leads, and exploring new opportunities.

In personal relationships, taking proactive steps to nurture the connection is essential. It means initiating meaningful conversations, planning activities or surprises for loved ones, and actively investing time and effort into the relationship. By taking the initiative, individuals demonstrate their commitment and dedication to the growth and happiness of their relationships.

In sales, professionals understand that different customers have unique preferences, needs, and communication styles. They adapt their approach accordingly to ensure effective engagement and relationship-building. In personal relationships, being flexible and adaptable allows individuals to accommodate the changing dynamics and evolving needs of their loved ones.

It means being open to new experiences, compromising when necessary, and finding common ground to maintain a harmonious and balanced relationship. A sales mentality in personal relationships emphasizes the importance of continuous improvement and self-reflection. In sales, professionals regularly evaluate their performance, seek feedback, and identify areas for growth. Applying this mindset to personal relationships involves introspection and self-awareness. Individuals can reflect on their communication style, strengths and weaknesses in relationships and actively work on improving themselves.

By committing to personal growth and self-improvement, individuals contribute to their personal relationships' overall health and vitality. Maintaining a sales mentality in personal relationships requires focusing on long-term relationship-building rather than short-term gains.

Likewise, personal relationships should focus on building strong foundations and nurturing long-term connections rather than seeking instant gratification. It means investing time, energy, and care into cultivating a deep and meaningful bond that withstands the test of time. A sales mentality in personal relationships emphasizes the power of gratitude and appreciation. In sales, professionals thank their customers for their business and loyalty. In personal relationships, expressing appreciation and gratitude to our loved ones for their presence, support, and love is essential. It fosters a sense of mutual appreciation, validates the efforts and contributions of both parties and creates a positive and uplifting environment for the relationship to flourish.

A sales mentality in personal relationships emphasizes the importance of authenticity and building trust. In sales, professionals strive to build trust with their customers by being honest, transparent, and delivering on their promises.

Being authentic, genuine, and trustworthy in personal relationships is crucial for establishing a deep and meaningful connection. By being true to oneself, demonstrating integrity, and honoring commitments, individuals lay the foundation of trust for healthy and thriving personal relationships.

Individuals can create and sustain strong, fulfilling, and harmonious personal relationships by being proactive, adaptable, self-reflective, focused on long-term relationship-building, expressing gratitude, managing conflicts effectively, and prioritizing authenticity and trust.

By applying the principles and strategies from the sales world, individuals can enhance their interpersonal skills, deepen connections, and foster a loving and supportive environment in their personal lives.

# Chapter 16: Using Sales Techniques to Overcome Fear and Self-Doubt

Fear and self-doubt are common obstacles hindering personal growth and limiting our potential. However, by harnessing sales techniques, we can effectively overcome these challenges and cultivate a mindset of confidence and success.

Chapter 16 explores how sales techniques can be applied to conquer fear and self-doubt, empowering individuals to reach new heights in their personal lives. Reframing is one powerful sales technique that can overcome fear and self-doubt. In sales, reframing involves shifting the perspective and focusing on the positive aspects of a situation rather than dwelling on the negative. In our personal lives, we can reframe our fears and self-doubts by viewing them as opportunities for growth and learning. Reframing our thoughts can transform fear into excitement and self-doubt into self-belief, allowing us to approach challenges with a more positive and proactive mindset.

Visualization is a powerful tool used by sales professionals to prepare themselves for success mentally. They build confidence and reduce anxiety by vividly imagining themselves achieving their goals and conquering obstacles. Likewise, we can employ visualization techniques to envision ourselves overcoming our fears and doubts in our personal lives. Visualizing ourselves confidently navigating challenging situations can boost our self-assurance and develop a resilient mindset. Goal setting is a crucial sales technique that can help us overcome fear and self-doubt.

In sales, professionals set specific, measurable, achievable, relevant, and time-bound (SMART) goals to stay focused and motivated. In our personal lives, setting clear and attainable goals gives us a sense of direction and purpose. By breaking down our fears and self-doubts into smaller, actionable goals, we can gradually chip away at them and build our confidence. Sales professionals understand the importance of preparation and practice.

They invest time in honing their skills, familiarizing themselves with their products or services, and rehearsing their sales pitches. In combating fear and self-doubt, preparation and practice play a crucial role. We can boost our confidence and alleviate anxiety by adequately preparing ourselves for challenging situations, whether a public speaking engagement or a difficult conversation. Practicing these scenarios beforehand can help us become more comfortable and competent, reducing the influence of fear and self-doubt.

A valuable sales technique that can be applied to conquer fear and self-doubt is the power of positive affirmations. Sales professionals often use affirmations to reinforce their belief in their abilities and maintain a positive mindset, in our personal lives, we can utilize positive affirmations to counteract negative self-talk and boost our self-confidence. By regularly affirming our strengths, talents, and potential, we reprogram our subconscious mind to focus on our capabilities rather than our limitations.

Adopting a growth mindset is paramount in overcoming fear and self-doubt. Sales professionals understand that setbacks and rejections are learning opportunities contribute to their growth and development. Embracing a growth mindset allows us to view failures and challenges as stepping stones to success. By reframing setbacks as valuable lessons, we can approach new situations with resilience, persistence, and a belief in our ability to overcome obstacles. Seeking support and guidance is crucial in overcoming fear and self-doubt.

Sales professionals often collaborate with mentors, attend training programs, and participate in peer-to-peer learning to enhance their skills and confidence. In our personal lives, reaching out for support can give us valuable insights, encouragement, and perspective. Surrounding ourselves with a supportive network of family, friends, or mentors who believe in us can bolster our self-assurance and help us navigate challenging times.

One effective sales technique that can be applied to conquer fear and self-doubt is the concept of the value proposition. In sales, professionals emphasize their product or service's unique value to potential customers. Similarly, in our personal lives, understanding our value proposition can help boost our confidence and combat self-doubt. By recognizing our strengths, talents, and the positive contributions, we bring to various situations. In sales, active prospecting involves proactively seeking out potential clients and initiating contact.

Actively seeking new opportunities and experiences can help us challenge our fears and build confidence. We expand our horizons and develop a more resilient mindset by stepping outside our comfort zones, engaging in new activities, and connecting with diverse individuals. The concept of objection handling in sales can be applied to overcome fear and self-doubt in our personal lives.

Professionals anticipate customer objections and prepare persuasive responses to address their concerns in sales. Preparing ourselves to face potential objections or criticism can help alleviate fear and boost our confidence. We can navigate challenging conversations and situations more effectively by arming ourselves with thoughtful responses and considering alternative perspectives. The sales technique of relationship building is crucial in overcoming fear and self-doubt. Professionals build trust, rapport, and long-term relationships with clients in sales. Nurturing meaningful connections with others can provide a support system and boost our confidence.

By cultivating strong relationships based on trust, empathy, and open communication, we create a supportive network that bolsters our self-belief and helps us navigate difficult times. The concept of continuous improvement in sales can be applied to conquer fear and self-doubt in our personal lives.

Sales professionals constantly learn, refine their skills, and adapt to changing market dynamics. Embracing a mindset of continuous improvement allows us to view challenges as opportunities for growth. By seeking out learning experiences, taking on new challenges, and embracing personal development, we expand our capabilities and become more resilient in fear and self-doubt.

This chapter highlights how sales techniques can be utilized to overcome fear and self-doubt in our personal lives. By leveraging concepts such as value proposition, active prospecting, objection handling, relationship building, continuous improvement, and resilience, we can gradually chip away at our fears, build self-confidence, and embrace new opportunities. Integrating these powerful sales techniques into our mindset and daily actions empowers us to conquer fear and self-doubt, unlocking our full potential and leading a more fulfilling life.

# Chapter 17: Sales and Setting and Achieving Personal Goals

Setting and achieving personal goals is fundamental to personal growth and success. It provides us with a sense of direction, purpose, and fulfilment. This explores the relationship between sales techniques and the effective process of setting and achieving personal goals. Sales professionals understand the importance of setting clear, specific, measurable goals.

They know their efforts may lack focus and direction without a well-defined target, leading to subpar results. Similarly, setting goals helps us establish a vision for what we want to accomplish and provides a roadmap for our journey. One sales technique that can be applied to personal goal setting is the concept of SMART goals.

By following this framework, we can create clear, quantifiable, realistic goals aligned with our values and priorities and have a specific timeframe for completion. Sales professionals also understand the importance of breaking down larger goals into smaller, manageable tasks. This technique, known as chunking, helps maintain motivation and allows for incremental progress.

In our personal lives, breaking goals into actionable steps keep us focused and prevents us from becoming overwhelmed. By celebrating small victories, we build momentum and drive towards our ultimate objectives. Sales professionals are skilled at tracking and measuring their progress. They use metrics and key performance indicators (KPIs) to evaluate their sales performance and adjust their strategies accordingly. Similarly, in personal goal setting, regular review and measurement are vital.

By assessing our progress, identifying areas for improvement, and making necessary adjustments, we stay on track and increase the likelihood of achieving our goals. Sales professionals often visualize themselves achieving success, closing deals, and surpassing their targets. They harness the power of visualization to boost motivation, build confidence, and create a positive mindset.

Similarly, in our personal lives, visualizing ourselves attaining our goals can fuel our determination, enhance our belief in our capabilities, and inspire us to take consistent action. Sales professionals also employ effective time management techniques to optimize their productivity. They prioritize tasks, eliminate distractions, and allocate time efficiently.

Similarly, in personal goal setting, managing our time effectively is crucial. By identifying our most important tasks, eliminating time-wasting activities, and creating a schedule that aligns with our goals, we maximize our productivity and make significant strides towards our desired outcomes. Sales professionals understand the importance of accountability. They often work in teams or report to managers who hold them accountable for their targets. This sense of responsibility drives their commitment and keeps them focused on their goals. Creating external accountability increases our commitment and motivation to follow through on our goals.

Sales professionals understand that setting and achieving personal goals is not a one-time event but an ongoing process. They recognize the importance of regularly reviewing and reassessing their goals to remain relevant and aligned with their evolving aspirations. Similarly, in our personal lives, we must periodically evaluate our goals and make any necessary adjustments to stay on track. Effective sales professionals continuously seek self-improvement. They invest in their personal and professional development by attending training programs, reading industry-related books, and seeking feedback from mentors or colleagues.

By continuously expanding our knowledge, acquiring new skills, and seeking personal growth opportunities, we enhance our abilities, broaden our perspectives, and increase our chances of achieving our goals. Collaboration is another skill that sales professionals excel at. They understand the importance of building relationships, fostering trust, and working with their colleagues and clients to achieve shared objectives.

In personal goal setting, collaboration can also play a significant role. Seeking support from others, whether it's through networking, finding accountability partners, or joining a mastermind group, can provide valuable insights, encouragement, and guidance as we strive towards our personal goals. Sales professionals recognize the significance of celebrating milestones and achievements along the way.

They acknowledge the value of acknowledging their progress and taking the time to celebrate their successes, no matter how small. In personal goal setting, celebrating milestones is equally crucial. By acknowledging and rewarding ourselves for our progress, we boost our motivation, reinforce positive habits, and maintain enthusiasm for the journey ahead. This chapter explores the application of sales techniques in setting and achieving personal goals.

By adopting flexibility, resilience, continuous self-improvement, collaboration, and celebrating milestones, we enhance our ability to navigate challenges, adapt to changing circumstances, and consistent progress towards our desired outcomes. Drawing inspiration from sales professionals, we can infuse our goal-setting journey with valuable strategies and mindsets, leading us to personal growth, fulfilment, and success.

# Chapter 18: The Role of Sales in Personal Development and Growth

Sales are not just about closing deals and generating revenue; it also profoundly impacts personal development and growth. The skills, mindsets, and strategies employed in the sales profession can be applied to various aspects of our lives, leading to personal growth, improved relationships, and increased self-confidence. In this chapter, we will explore the transformative role of sales in personal development and how it can contribute to our overall growth.

One of the key areas where sales can positively influence personal development is communication skills. Effective communication lies at the heart of sales success, and by honing our communication abilities, we can enhance our personal and professional relationships. Sales professionals are skilled at articulating their thoughts, actively listening to others, and adapting their communication styles to connect with different individuals.

By adopting these communication techniques in our personal lives, we can improve our ability to express ourselves, understand others, and foster meaningful connections. Sales also require resilience and the ability to handle rejection.

In the sales profession, rejection is common, and salespeople must develop a thick skin to bounce back from setbacks and keep moving forward. This resilience can be applied to personal development as well. By embracing the mindset of resilience, we become more equipped to handle failures, setbacks, and challenges in various aspects of our lives.

We learn to view setbacks as opportunities for growth, to persevere in the face of adversity, and to maintain a positive outlook even when things don't go as planned. Sales professionals understand the importance of setting and working towards goals with focus and determination. They set targets, create action plans, and track their progress meticulously.

This goal-oriented approach can be transformative in personal development. By adopting a similar mindset and applying goal-setting techniques in our personal lives, we become more intentional about our growth and progress. We identify areas for improvement, set meaningful goals, and take consistent action towards achieving them.

This sense of purpose and direction propels us forward and enables us to make significant strides in personal development. Sales also teach us the value of continuous learning and self-improvement. Successful sales professionals invest time and effort in expanding their knowledge, staying updated on industry trends, and sharpening their skills. This dedication to ongoing learning can be applied to personal development as well.

By embracing a growth mindset and actively seeking opportunities for learning and self-improvement, we open ourselves up to new possibilities, develop new skills, and broaden our horizons. This commitment to personal growth enhances our capabilities and fuels our passion and enthusiasm for life.

Moreover, sales often involve problem-solving and finding creative solutions to meet clients' needs. This problem-solving mindset can be invaluable in personal development. By approaching challenges and obstacles with a problem-solving mindset, we become more resourceful, adaptable, and proactive in finding solutions.

We learn to think outside the box, consider alternative perspectives, and overcome obstacles with resilience and determination. Sales professionals can uniquely understand and empathize with clients' needs and desires. They excel at putting themselves in their customers' shoes and finding tailored solutions to their challenges. This empathetic approach is not limited to sales transactions alone. It can be applied to personal relationships, allowing us to develop a deeper understanding of others and build stronger connections.

By cultivating empathy in our personal lives, we become more compassionate, sensitive, and supportive, fostering harmonious relationships and nurturing a sense of community.

Sales also require effective time management and organizational skills. Salespeople must prioritize tasks, manage their schedules, and stay on top of deadlines. These skills can be invaluable in personal development, helping us become more efficient and productive.

By mastering time management techniques, we can optimize our daily routines, balance work and personal life, and allocate time for self-care, hobbies, and personal growth pursuits. This disciplined approach enables us to make the most of our time, achieve our goals, and experience a sense of fulfilment in both our professional and personal endeavors.

Sales professionals often encounter a diverse range of clients, each with their own unique preferences, communication styles, and decision-making processes. By developing adaptability and flexibility, we become more adept at navigating various social contexts and interacting with different personality types.

This adaptability spills over into our personal lives, allowing us to navigate social settings, handle conflicts, and build rapport with individuals from diverse backgrounds. It broadens our perspective, fosters open-mindedness, and enhances our ability to connect with various people. Sales also teach us the importance of resilience and perseverance.

In the face of rejections, objections, and setbacks, sales professionals must maintain a positive attitude and keep pushing forward. This resilience is crucial in personal development as well. Life is filled with challenges and obstacles, and our ability to bounce back from failures and setbacks determines our personal growth.

By cultivating resilience, we develop a strong mindset to overcome adversity, learn from our experiences, and emerge stronger and wiser. Sales encourage a proactive and results-oriented mindset. Salespeople are driven by targets and goals, constantly seeking ways to improve their performance and achieve better outcomes.

This proactive approach can be applied to personal development as we set goals and take proactive steps to reach them. Whether pursuing a new hobby, learning a new skill, or making positive lifestyle changes, adopting a results-oriented mindset enables us to take ownership of our growth journey and actively work towards becoming the best version of ourselves.

Sales also provide opportunities for continuous feedback and self-reflection. Sales professionals receive feedback from clients, managers, and colleagues, allowing them to identify areas for improvement and refine their strategies. Personal development requires self-reflection and the willingness to seek feedback from trusted individuals.

By embracing feedback and self-reflection, we gain valuable insights into our strengths, weaknesses, and areas for growth. This self-awareness empowers us to make meaningful changes, develop new habits, and continuously evolve on our personal development journey.

Sales influence our professional lives and significantly influence personal development and growth. The skills, mindsets, and strategies learned in sales can be applied to enhancing our relationships, time management abilities, adaptability, resilience, proactive mindset, and self-reflection.

By integrating the lessons from sales into our personal development journey, we can unlock our potential, foster personal growth, and lead more fulfilling and purposeful lives.

# Chapter 19: How Sales and Marketing Overlap in Your Everyday Life

Sales and marketing are two closely intertwined disciplines that work together to drive business success. While they are distinct fields, their influence extends beyond the corporate world. Sales and marketing techniques and principles are omnipresent in our daily lives, shaping our choices, influencing our behaviors, and guiding our decision-making processes. Marketing is about understanding customer needs and wants and creating effective strategies to meet those needs. This involves identifying target audiences, conducting market research, and developing compelling messaging and branding.

In our everyday lives, we encounter marketing efforts all around us. From television commercials to social media advertisements, and billboards to product packaging, marketing messages are designed to capture our attention, pique our interest, and persuade us to act. Consider how marketing impacts our purchasing decisions. When we browse a store, we are bombarded with product displays, promotional offers, and enticing packaging.

These are all strategic marketing tactics to capture our attention and influence our buying behavior. From carefully crafted product descriptions to visually appealing designs, marketing plays a pivotal role in shaping our perceptions of products and brands. Marketing extends beyond the realm of traditional advertising. It encompasses content marketing, influencer marketing, experiential marketing, and more.

Consider how you come across blog posts, articles, and videos offering advice, tips, and insights on various topics. Brands or individuals often create content to establish their expertise, build trust, and influence consumer behavior. Influencer marketing, on the other hand, leverages the power of influential individuals to promote products or services. Influencers, whether celebrities, industry experts, or social media personalities, have built a dedicated following who trust their recommendations.

By partnering with influencers, brands can tap into their audience and leverage their credibility and influence to drive sales. Experiential marketing focuses on creating immersive and memorable experiences that leave a lasting impact on consumers. Think about events, product demonstrations, or interactive campaigns allowing consumers to engage with a brand personally. These experiences evoke emotions, create positive associations, and deepen the connection between consumers and brands.

On the other hand, sales are the art of closing deals and generating revenue. While marketing lays the groundwork for sales by creating awareness and interest, sales professionals are responsible for converting that interest into actual purchases. Sales techniques, such as consultative selling, relationship building, and effective communication, are crucial in convincing potential customers to buy. In our everyday lives, sales techniques are present in various scenarios. We employ sales skills when we negotiate a better price for a car, persuade a friend to join us for a movie, or convince our family to try a new restaurant. These skills involve listening actively, understanding needs, presenting compelling arguments, addressing objections, and closing the deal. The overlap between sales and marketing is evident in our interactions with businesses and individuals.

Marketing creates the initial interest and sets the stage, while sales professionals utilize their skills to guide us through decision-making and facilitate the transaction. This symbiotic relationship between sales and marketing is crucial for businesses to thrive as they work together to attract customers, build relationships, and drive revenue. Sales and marketing are ubiquitous in our everyday lives. Whether we realize it or not, we are constantly exposed to marketing messages and influenced by sales techniques. From the products we buy to the experiences we engage in, sales and marketing play a significant role in shaping our choices and behaviors.

# Chapter 20: Understanding the Customer Lifecycle in Your Personal Life

The customer lifecycle is a concept widely utilized in business and marketing to understand and manage the various stages a customer goes through in their relationship with a company. It encompasses the journey from initial awareness and consideration of a product or service to the post-purchase stage and beyond.

While typically applied in a business context, the principles of the customer lifecycle can also be valuable in our personal lives, helping us navigate relationships, make informed decisions, and foster meaningful connections. The first stage of the customer lifecycle is awareness. This is when a customer becomes aware of a product or service and begins to gather information. In our personal lives, awareness plays a crucial role in our relationships. We become aware of potential partners, friends, or social groups through various channels such as social events, introductions, or online platforms. This stage is characterized by curiosity, exploration, and gathering initial impressions.

Next comes the consideration stage, where the customer evaluates the available options and weighs the pros and cons of each. In our personal lives, this stage relates to getting to know someone on a deeper level. We consider their values, interests, compatibility, and shared experiences to determine if a connection or relationship is worth pursuing. This stage involves thoughtful reflection and discernment.

Once a customer has decided and purchased, they enter the acquisition stage. In this phase, the customer becomes active, engaging with the product or service and experiencing its benefits firsthand. Similarly, in personal relationships, this stage signifies the beginning of a deeper connection. It involves spending time together, building shared experiences, and discovering the value and joy that the relationship brings.

As time progresses, customers may reach the retention stage, where they continue to engage with the product or service over an extended period. This stage reflects the commitment and effort put into nurturing and maintaining the connection in personal relationships. It involves building trust, effective communication, and shared growth. The retention stage is essential for long-term satisfaction and fulfilment in business and personal relationships.

However, just as customers can reach the end of their journey with a product or service, personal relationships can also face an ending or transition. This stage, known as the churn or disengagement stage in business, signifies the end of the relationship. In personal life, it could be a breakup, the drifting apart of friends, or the natural conclusion of a phase in life. It's important to recognize that endings are a natural part of life and provide opportunities for growth, reflection, and new beginnings.

Understanding the customer lifecycle in our personal lives helps us navigate relationships with intention and clarity. It allows us to assess our needs, make informed choices, and invest time and energy in meaningful connections. Recognizing the different stages and dynamics, we can manage expectations, communicate effectively, and foster healthy and fulfilling relationships. It's essential to recognize how marketing principles overlap with our everyday lives. Marketing is not limited to business contexts alone; it influences our personal lives in various ways.

Recognizing these overlaps allows us to navigate our personal experiences more effectively and make informed decisions. One area where sales and marketing overlap in our everyday lives is personal branding. Just as companies develop a brand image to differentiate themselves, individuals can also cultivate a personal brand. Personal branding involves consciously crafting and communicating our unique identity, values, and expertise to make a positive impression on others. This can be particularly valuable in professional settings, networking events, or job interviews, where we want to leave a lasting impact and stand out.

Marketing principles can be applied to social relationships and networking. Building and maintaining relationships require effective communication, trust, and relationship-building skills. By understanding marketing principles, such as segmentation, targeting, and positioning, we can tailor our interactions to specific individuals or groups. This involves recognizing their needs, interests, and preferences and adjusting our approach accordingly. Doing so can establish meaningful connections and foster mutually beneficial relationships.

Another area where sales and marketing intersect in our personal lives is persuasion and influence. Marketing techniques, such as persuasive messaging and storytelling, can be applied to personal situations where we seek to convince or influence others. Whether it's persuading a friend to try a new activity, convincing a family member to support a cause, or negotiating a decision within a group, the principles of sales and marketing can be valuable tools.

By understanding the motivations and needs of others, we can tailor our messages and arguments to resonate with them, increasing the likelihood of successful persuasion. The principles of marketing can help us in managing our finances. Budgeting, saving, and making wise financial decisions are essential aspects of our lives.

We can make informed choices when purchasing products or services by applying marketing concepts like market research and comparison shopping. We can evaluate different options, consider their value and benefits, and make financial decisions that align with our goals and priorities. By taking a strategic approach to our finances, we can optimize our resources and work towards long-term financial well-being.

Understanding the customer lifecycle and marketing principles can also benefit our personal growth and self-improvement. As businesses strive to understand their customer's needs and provide solutions, we can apply a similar mindset to our personal development. We can evolve and grow as individuals by conducting self-assessments, setting goals, and continuously learning and adapting. This customer-centric approach to personal growth allows us to identify areas for improvement, seek relevant resources and support, and track our progress over time.

The overlap between sales, marketing, and our personal lives is significant. By recognizing these connections, we can apply principles from the world of business to enhance our personal experiences. From personal branding and relationship-building to persuasion and financial decision-making, the insights and strategies derived from sales and marketing can empower us to navigate our personal lives more effectively and make informed choices. By embracing these principles, we can enhance our personal growth, build meaningful connections, and achieve greater fulfilment and success in our everyday lives.

# Chapter 21: The Importance of Branding in Your Personal Life

Branding is important in many aspects of our lives, not just businesses and products. Just as companies strive to establish a strong brand identity, individuals can benefit from understanding and harnessing the power of personal branding. Building a personal brand has become increasingly important in today's interconnected world, where personal reputation and online presence are highly influential.

One of the key aspects of personal branding is creating a clear and authentic identity. This involves identifying and articulating our unique values, passions, strengths, and expertise. By understanding what sets us apart, we can develop a personal brand that reflects our true essence. This authenticity is crucial in establishing trust and building meaningful connections with others, personally and professionally.

Personal branding allows us to differentiate ourselves in a crowded and competitive world. Just as companies aim to stand out from their competitors, individuals can use personal branding to highlight their unique qualities and attract opportunities. By cultivating a strong personal brand, we can position ourselves as experts or thought leaders in our respective fields, making us more visible and memorable to others. This can open doors to new relationships, career opportunities, and personal growth.

In the digital age, online presence has become integral to personal branding. Social media platforms, personal websites, and online portfolios serve as channels for showcasing our brand and connecting with a wider audience. Curating our online presence carefully is essential, ensuring that it aligns with our brand and conveys the desired image. Consistency across different online platforms and maintaining professionalism in our digital interactions contribute to a strong personal brand. Personal branding also extends to how we present ourselves offline, such as in networking events, social gatherings, or professional settings.

Our appearance, communication style, and personal interactions shape the perception others have of us. By being mindful of these aspects and aligning them with our brand, we can make a positive impression and leave a lasting impact on others. When our brand is well-defined and communicated effectively, it acts as a magnet, attracting people and opportunities that resonate with who we are. We can attract like-minded individuals, collaborations, and meaningful projects by showcasing our expertise, sharing our knowledge, and expressing our values. This helps us build a fulfilling and purpose-driven personal and professional life. Personal branding can contribute to personal growth and self-awareness.

As we develop our brand, we engage in self-reflection and introspection. We assess our strengths, weaknesses, and areas for improvement. This self-awareness enables us to set meaningful goals, pursue personal development opportunities, and work towards becoming the best version of ourselves. We embark on self-discovery and growth by continuously refining and evolving our brand. Personal branding empowers us to take control of our narrative and shape how others perceive us.

Instead of leaving our reputation and personal image to chance, we can intentionally craft and manage our brand. By proactively showcasing our achievements, sharing our expertise, and engaging in authentic and meaningful conversations, we can influence how others perceive us. This control over our narrative helps us build trust, credibility, and influence in our personal and professional relationships.

Personal branding extends beyond establishing a strong reputation; it also involves creating a compelling story around our brand. Our narrative is the thread that weaves together our experiences, values, and aspirations, giving our brand a distinct voice and meaning. We can engage others deeper, inspire them, and create a lasting impact by crafting a compelling story.

One aspect of personal branding often overlooked is the importance of consistent personal values. Our values serve as guiding principles that shape our decisions, behaviors, and interactions. When our brand aligns with our core values, we create a sense of authenticity and integrity that resonates with others. This alignment strengthens our brand and enhances our overall well-being and satisfaction in life.

Just as businesses rely on a strong network of clients and partners, individuals can benefit from cultivating a supportive and diverse network. By connecting with like-minded individuals, mentors, and influencers, we expand our opportunities, gain valuable insights, and receive support and encouragement in our personal and professional endeavors. Personal branding also involves continuously adapting and evolving to stay relevant and impactful. The world and our goals, interests, and skills are constantly changing.

To maintain a strong personal brand, we must be open to learning, growth, and embracing new challenges. This may involve acquiring new knowledge, developing new skills, or exploring new areas of interest. By staying agile and adaptable, we ensure that our brand remains dynamic and relevant in a rapidly evolving world.

Personal branding can also lead to increased self-confidence and empowerment. We become more self-assured in our interactions and decisions when we clearly understand our brand and its value. We project confidence and conviction, attracting others and creating opportunities for collaboration and success.

Personal branding empowers us to own our unique strengths and capabilities, enabling us to achieve our goals with greater confidence and resilience. Personal branding is not just about self-promotion; it also involves adding value to others. We build trust and credibility by focusing on providing value and serving others. We became a valuable resource and trusted authority in our respective domains by sharing our knowledge, insights, and resources. This mindset of adding value fosters a positive and collaborative environment where everyone can thrive and succeed together.

Personal branding is a powerful tool that goes beyond establishing a reputation. It involves crafting a compelling story, aligning with our values, building meaningful relationships, embracing growth and adaptation, and adding value to others. By investing in our brand, we can create a positive and authentic presence that attracts opportunities, fosters connections, and enables us to live a purpose-driven and fulfilling life. Personal branding empowers us to shape our narrative, build confidence, and make a meaningful impact in our personal and professional spheres.

# Chapter 22: Maintaining Work-Life Balance as a Salesperson

Any professional's performance and well-being depend on maintaining a decent work-life balance, but salespeople, in particular, must do so. In the fast-paced and demanding sales world, striking a harmonious balance between work responsibilities and personal life can be challenging. However, achieving a sense of equilibrium and fulfilment in both domains is possible with the right mindset, strategies, and boundaries.

Sales professionals often face tight deadlines, high-pressure situations, and constant tasks and responsibilities. Salespeople can ensure they utilize their time effectively and efficiently by prioritizing and organizing tasks, setting realistic goals, and allocating time for essential activities. This allows them to complete their work efficiently and creates space for personal activities and downtime.

Establishing clear boundaries between work and personal life is another essential aspect of maintaining balance. Salespeople often find themselves constantly connected to work through technology and communication channels. While it is crucial to be accessible and responsive to clients and colleagues, setting limits and carving out dedicated time for personal life are equally important.

This may involve creating designated "no-work" zones or periods, such as evenings or weekends, where work-related activities are minimized or avoided altogether. By setting boundaries, salespeople can protect their time and recharge, increasing productivity and satisfaction in both professional and personal spheres. Practicing self-care is another vital component of work-life balance for salespeople.

The high-stress nature of sales can take a toll on mental, emotional, and physical well-being. Engaging in activities that promote relaxation, rejuvenation, and self-care is essential for maintaining resilience and avoiding burnout. This may include regular exercise, mindfulness practices, hobbies and pursuing personal interests. By prioritizing self-care, salespeople can replenish their energy, reduce stress, and approach work and personal life with renewed vigor and enthusiasm.

Creating a support system is also crucial for maintaining a work-life balance. Salespeople can benefit from a network of trusted colleagues, mentors, and friends who understand their profession's unique challenges and demands. Sharing experiences, seeking advice, and receiving emotional support from this network can help salespeople navigate the ups and downs of their careers while maintaining a healthy perspective.

Involving family members and loved ones in open and honest communication about work demands can foster understanding and support, further contributing to a balanced and harmonious life. Effective stress management techniques are essential for salespeople to thrive professionally and personally. Sales can be an unpredictable and high-pressure environment, and stress is an inevitable part of the job. Finding healthy and constructive ways to manage stress is critical for preventing it from spilling over into personal life.

This may involve techniques such as deep breathing exercises, meditation, engaging in hobbies, seeking counselling or therapy, and practicing positive self-talk. By proactively managing stress, salespeople can maintain mental and emotional well-being and navigate challenges with resilience and grace. Leveraging technology and automation tools can streamline work processes and save salespeople valuable time.

Embracing customer relationship management (CRM) systems, sales analytics software, and other productivity tools can help automate repetitive tasks, streamline workflows, and enhance efficiency. By maximizing technology's potential, salespeople can optimize their work processes and create more time and space for personal life.

Salespeople need to evaluate their priorities, goals, and values periodically. As career aspirations and personal circumstances evolve, it is necessary to reassess whether the current work-life balance aligns with these changes. This reflection can help salespeople make necessary adjustments, set new boundaries, and realign their efforts to ensure ongoing balance and fulfilment. Developing strong communication skills is crucial for maintaining a work-life balance as a salesperson.

Effective communication enables salespeople to clearly express their needs, set expectations, and negotiate boundaries with clients and colleagues. By practicing assertiveness and open communication, salespeople can avoid overcommitting themselves, prevent work from encroaching on personal time, and foster a healthy work environment.

This skill is valuable in sales and personal relationships, as it promotes understanding, mutual respect, and effective conflict resolution. Flexibility and adaptability are also key qualities for salespeople striving to maintain work-life balance. The sales profession often requires flexibility in terms of working hours, travel, and unexpected changes in plans.

By cultivating a flexible mindset and embracing adaptability, salespeople can navigate work demands while accommodating personal commitments and priorities. This flexibility extends beyond work-related situations and can be applied to personal life, allowing for greater agility in managing responsibilities and pursuing personal goals.

Networking and professional development opportunities can play a significant role in achieving work-life balance as a salesperson. Building connections with industry peers and attending conferences, workshops, or seminars enhances professional growth and provides valuable insights and strategies for managing work-life integration.

By staying connected with like-minded professionals and staying informed about industry trends, salespeople can learn from others' experiences, gain fresh perspectives, and discover innovative approaches to balancing their personal and professional lives.

Salespeople can benefit from delegating tasks and seeking support when needed. The ability to delegate effectively allows salespeople to focus on their core responsibilities while entrusting others with tasks that can be handled by colleagues or support staff. By utilizing teamwork and collaboration, salespeople can offload some workloads and create space for personal life.

Delegating also fosters a sense of trust and empowerment within the team, enhancing overall productivity and work satisfaction.

A holistic approach to work-life balance involves aligning personal values and purpose with professional pursuits. Salespeople who find meaning and purpose in their work are likelier to experience a sense of fulfilment and balance in their lives. Understanding personal values and how they align with career goals can help salespeople prioritize activities and opportunities that resonate with their core beliefs.

Salespeople can find greater satisfaction and fulfilment by pursuing work that aligns with personal values, leading to a more harmonious integration of work and personal life. Salespeople need to practice self-reflection and self-care regularly.

Taking time to assess personal needs, desires, and aspirations allows salespeople to make conscious choices and take intentional actions to support their well-being. This may include engaging in activities that promote physical and mental health, setting boundaries to protect personal time, and seeking personal growth and development opportunities outside of work.

Maintaining work-life balance as a salesperson is an ongoing journey that requires a proactive and mindful approach. Salespeople can foster a harmonious integration of their personal and professional lives by honing communication skills, cultivating flexibility, seeking networking and professional development opportunities, delegating tasks, aligning values with work, and practicing self-reflection and self-care.

Striving for work-life balance enhances personal well-being and contributes to long-term success and fulfilment in the sales profession.

By embracing these strategies, salespeople can lead meaningful and balanced lives, achieving success inside and outside their careers.

# Chapter 23: Sales Lessons for a Happy and Successful Personal Life

Sales skills are valuable in business and can be applied to different aspects of our personal lives. The principles of effective selling, such as building relationships, understanding needs, and providing solutions, can contribute to a happy and successful personal life. This chapter explores how sales lessons can be applied to personal relationships, goal achievement, personal growth, and overall well-being.

One important sales lesson that can enhance personal relationships is the art of building rapport. Salespeople understand the importance of establishing connections and building trust with their clients. We can create deeper connections and strengthen our bonds by actively listening, showing empathy, and demonstrating genuine interest in others.

In sales, it is crucial to identify potential customers' pain points and desires and provide tailored solutions. Similarly, in our personal lives, taking the time to understand the needs, desires, and aspirations of those around us can help us support and uplift them. By offering our time, assistance, or simply lending a listening ear, we can contribute to the well-being and happiness of our loved ones.

Goal setting and achievement is another area where sales techniques can be applied to personal life. Salespeople are adept at setting clear, measurable goals and developing strategies. By adopting a similar approach in our personal lives, we can identify our aspirations and create actionable plans to turn them into reality.

Whether pursuing a new hobby, advancing in our careers, or improving our health, setting clear goals and implementing sales-inspired strategies like prospecting, follow-up, and perseverance can propel us towards success.

Effective communication is a cornerstone of successful sales and vital in personal relationships. Salespeople understand the power of clear, concise, and persuasive communication to influence others. Effective communication techniques, such as active listening, clarity, and empathy, can greatly enhance our interactions.

By effectively expressing our thoughts and emotions, we can prevent misunderstandings, resolve conflicts, and foster harmony in our relationships. Salespeople are often skilled in negotiation, which is valuable in professional and personal contexts.

Negotiation skills can help us navigate differences, find common ground, and reach mutually beneficial outcomes.

Whether negotiating with a partner, discussing a family matter, or making decisions with friends, employing sales-inspired negotiation techniques such as understanding interests, exploring alternatives, and finding win-win solutions can lead to healthier and more satisfying relationships.

Personal growth and development are areas where sales lessons can significantly impact. Salespeople are continuously learning and improving their skills to stay competitive. Similarly, in our personal lives, embracing a growth mindset and seeking opportunities for learning and self-improvement can lead to personal fulfilment and success.

By attending workshops, reading books, seeking mentors, and stepping outside our comfort zones, we can expand our knowledge, develop new skills, and unlock our full potential. Salespeople understand the importance of resilience and perseverance in facing challenges and rejection. In personal life, setbacks and obstacles are inevitable, but adopting a sales-inspired mindset of resilience can help us overcome them.

By viewing failures as learning opportunities, staying motivated, and persisting towards our goals, we can navigate life's ups and downs with greater resilience and ultimately achieve greater happiness and success. Salespeople recognize the significance of self-care and work-life balance.

They understand the importance of managing stress, taking breaks, and prioritizing their well-being. In our personal lives, practicing self-care, setting boundaries, and creating a healthy work-life balance is crucial for our overall happiness and satisfaction.

By dedicating time to activities that recharge us, nurturing our physical and mental health, and valuing our personal needs, we can lead more fulfilling lives and better support those around us. Sales professionals understand the importance of adaptability and agility in an ever-changing market. They quickly embrace new technologies, strategies, and trends to stay ahead of the competition.

Similarly, being adaptable and open to change in our personal lives allows us to navigate life's transitions and challenges more effectively. Whether adjusting to a new job, moving to a different city, or adapting to unforeseen circumstances, adopting a sales-inspired mindset of flexibility enables us to embrace change and thrive in uncertainty. Sales also teach us the value of resilience and perseverance.

Salespeople often face rejection, objections, and setbacks but maintain a positive attitude. This resilience can be applied in our personal lives when we encounter obstacles or face adversity. By maintaining a growth mindset, learning from failures, and staying determined, we can overcome challenges and emerge stronger. Resilience allows us to bounce back from setbacks and pursue personal goals and aspirations.

Sales professionals understand the importance of continuous relationship-building and nurturing. They know that maintaining long-term relationships with clients is key to success. This principle can be extended to our personal lives as well.

Cultivating and nurturing relationships with family, friends, and partners requires consistent effort, communication, and care. By investing time and energy into our connections, we can build strong and supportive networks that enrich our lives and provide a sense of belonging and fulfilment. Sales also emphasize the significance of self-motivation and self-discipline.

Targets, goals, and incentives often drive salespeople, and they have the discipline to work independently and stay focused. These principles in our personal lives can help us stay motivated and disciplined when pursuing personal projects or self-improvement endeavors.

We can progress and achieve desired outcomes by setting personal goals, creating action plans, and holding ourselves accountable. The techniques employed in sales have far-reaching applications in our personal lives.

By incorporating the lessons learned from sales, such as effective decision-making, adaptability, resilience, relationship-building, self-motivation, storytelling, and continuous learning, we can elevate our personal experiences and lead more fulfilling and successful lives.

The skills and mindset cultivated through sales can empower us to overcome challenges, forge meaningful connections, achieve our goals, and embrace personal growth. Sales lessons offer valuable insights that can positively impact our lives and contribute to our well-being and happiness.

# Chapter 24: Bouncing Back from Sales and Personal Setbacks

Life is full of ups and downs, and sales professionals and individuals encounter setbacks and disappointments. In the sales world, rejection, lost deals, and missed targets are common occurrences. However, what sets successful salespeople apart is their ability to bounce back from setbacks and turn failures into opportunities for growth. This resilience and determination can also be applied to our personal lives, enabling us to navigate disappointment and setbacks with grace and resilience.

It's natural to feel frustrated, discouraged, or even defeated when things don't go as planned. However, dwelling on negative emotions or blaming external factors won't help us progress. Instead, by accepting the situation and taking responsibility for our reactions and actions, we gain the power to regain control over our lives.

Next, reflecting on the setback and learning from it is important. Sales professionals often conduct post-mortems or debriefings to analyze what went wrong in a sales process. Similarly, we can benefit from introspection and evaluation in our personal lives. By asking ourselves questions such as "What could I have done differently?" or "What lessons can I take away from this experience?" we gain valuable insights that can guide our decisions and actions. This reflection allows us to grow and improve, turning setbacks into opportunities for personal development. Another key aspect of bouncing back is maintaining a positive mindset., Cultivating a positive mindset can help us overcome disappointment and setbacks.

By focusing on the lessons learned, the growth opportunities, and the possibilities for a brighter future, we can shift our perspective and find the motivation to keep moving forward. Positive self-talk, gratitude practices, and surrounding ourselves with supportive individuals can further enhance our resilience and help us bounce back stronger than ever. It's also crucial to seek support during challenging times. Sales professionals often rely on their colleagues, mentors, or coaches for guidance and encouragement.

In our personal lives, having a strong support system is equally important. Whether seeking advice from a trusted friend, confiding in a family member, or professional help from a therapist or counsellor, reaching out for support can provide us with the necessary emotional and practical assistance to navigate setbacks.

Surrounding ourselves with positive, understanding individuals who believe in our abilities can boost our confidence and resilience. Setting new goals and creating a roadmap for the future can help us regain focus and motivation. In the sales world, professionals often set new targets or redefine their strategies after facing setbacks.

Setting new goals and creating a plan of action can give us a sense of purpose and direction. Whether pursuing a new career path, embarking on a personal project, or reevaluating our priorities, having a clear vision for the future can reignite our passion and drive. It's important to maintain perspective and embrace a growth mindset.

Likewise, in our personal lives, setbacks and disappointments are part of the human experience. We can approach these challenges with a sense of resilience and optimism by viewing them as opportunities for growth and personal development. Embracing a growth mindset allows us to see setbacks as valuable lessons and stepping stones toward a more fulfilling and successful life.

Bouncing back from sales setbacks and personal life disappointments also requires adaptability and flexibility. In the dynamic world of sales, professionals often encounter unexpected changes in the market, shifts in customer preferences, or disruptive technologies. Unforeseen circumstances, unexpected challenges, or relationship changes can impact our plans and goals. By developing adaptability and embracing flexibility, we can navigate these changes resiliently and find new opportunities amidst the setbacks.

One way to cultivate adaptability is by staying informed and continuously learning. Sales professionals understand the importance of staying updated on industry trends, market dynamics, and our personal lives; being open to learning and acquiring new knowledge can help us adapt to changing circumstances.

This may involve reading books, attending workshops or seminars, taking online courses, or seeking mentorship from individuals who have faced similar challenges. By expanding our knowledge and skills, we become better equipped to handle setbacks and make informed decisions for our personal growth. Sales professionals often face rejection and encounter skepticism from potential clients. However, their unwavering self-belief in their product, service, or themselves enables them to persevere and overcome obstacles. In our personal lives, building self-confidence and nurturing self-belief are equally important.

By recognizing our strengths, acknowledging our achievements, and cultivating a positive self-image, we develop the inner resilience to bounce back from disappointments. This involves practicing self-affirmation, celebrating small wins, and surrounding ourselves with positive influences that uplift and support our journey.

Maintaining a solution-oriented mindset can contribute to bouncing back from setbacks. Sales professionals are adept at finding creative solutions to meet customer needs and overcome objects in our personal lives; adopting a solution-oriented approach allows us to focus on finding alternatives and taking proactive steps to address challenges. Instead of dwelling on the problem, we channel our energy into brainstorming ideas, seeking advice, and taking action. This proactive mindset helps us regain control and move forward with purpose.

Bouncing back from sales setbacks and personal life disappointments requires adaptability, self-belief, a solution-oriented mindset, resilience-building techniques, seeking inspiration from others, and practicing self-compassion.

By embracing these qualities, we can navigate challenges, learn from setbacks, and emerge stronger and more resilient. Remember, setbacks are not indicators of failure but growth and personal development opportunities.

# Chapter 25: Using Sales Skills to Fundraise and Raise Awareness for Nonprofits

Fundraising and raising awareness for nonprofits are essential activities that rely on effective communication, relationship-building, and persuasion skills. Chapter 25 explores how sales skills can be leveraged to support nonprofit organizations and make a meaningful impact in the community. Just as sales professionals craft narratives that resonate with their target audience, nonprofit fundraisers need to communicate the mission and impact of their organization compellingly. By sharing stories of individuals or communities positively affected by the nonprofit's work, fundraisers can engage potential donors and inspire them to contribute.

In addition to storytelling, building strong relationships is crucial in fundraising. Sales professionals understand the importance of cultivating trust and rapport with their clients, and the same principles apply to nonprofit fundraising. Developing authentic connections with donors involves active listening, empathy, and understanding their philanthropic motivations. By building genuine relationships, fundraisers can establish long-term partnerships and create a sense of loyalty and commitment to the nonprofit's cause.

Persuasive communication is a vital skill in both sales and fundraising. Sales professionals are adept at presenting the value proposition of their products or services, addressing objections, and influencing purchasing decisions.

Nonprofit fundraisers need to convey the impact and value of their organization's work to potential donors. This requires clear and compelling communication that highlights the difference their contributions can make in the lives of those in need. Sales professionals often employ various techniques to overcome objections and close deals, and these techniques can be adapted to fundraising as well.

Understanding donors' potential objections or concerns allows fundraisers to address them and provide reassurance proactively. Funders can increase the likelihood of securing donations by anticipating objections and presenting compelling counterarguments. Leveraging networking skills can be instrumental in fundraising. Sales professionals understand the power of building a strong network and tapping into existing connections to expand their customer base.

Nonprofit fundraisers can leverage their personal and professional networks to expand the reach of their fundraising efforts. Networking events, social gatherings, and community engagements provide opportunities to connect with individuals who share a passion for philanthropy and may be interested in supporting the cause. Sales professionals often use data and analytics to inform their strategies and optimize their sales processes.

Nonprofit fundraisers can leverage data to identify potential donors, tailor their fundraising appeals, and measure the impact of their efforts. Funders can design targeted campaigns that resonate with specific segments of their donor base by analyzing donor preferences, giving patterns, and market trends. Sales skills can also be applied to raising awareness for nonprofits.

Sales professionals understand the importance of brand visibility and developing effective marketing strategies to reach their target audience. Nonprofit organizations can benefit from similar tactics by utilizing social media, content marketing, and public relations to raise awareness about their cause and engage with the community. Sales professionals often participate in continuous professional development to enhance their skills and stay updated on industry trends. Nonprofit fundraisers can also benefit from ongoing training and education to refine their fundraising techniques, learn new strategies, and stay informed about best practices in the nonprofit sector.

By investing in their professional development, fundraisers can continuously improve their effectiveness and make a greater impact in their fundraising efforts. Like sales professionals celebrate milestones and achievements, nonprofit organizations should recognize and appreciate their donors.

Expressing gratitude and providing regular updates on the impact of donations creates a sense of involvement and satisfaction for donors. This can foster long-term relationships and encourage continued support for the nonprofit's mission. Another valuable sales skill that can be applied to fundraising and nonprofit work is identifying and understanding potential donors' needs and motivations.

Sales professionals are skilled at conducting thorough research and gathering insights about their target audience to tailor their sales pitches effectively. Nonprofit fundraisers can benefit from conducting donor research to understand potential supporters' interests, values, and philanthropic goals.

This information can help fundraisers customize their appeals and establish meaningful connections with donors based on shared interests and passions. Sales professionals often employ effective time management and prioritization techniques to optimize productivity.

This skill is equally important for nonprofit fundraisers who often juggle multiple fundraising campaigns, events, and administrative tasks. By utilizing time management strategies such as setting goals, prioritizing activities, and leveraging technology tools, fundraisers can enhance their efficiency and effectiveness in achieving fundraising targets. Sales professionals understand the value of building a strong personal brand and establishing themselves as trusted experts. This principle applies to nonprofit fundraisers as well.

Cultivating a strong personal brand as a fundraiser can help inspire confidence and trust among potential donors. By demonstrating expertise, passion, and a track record of successful fundraising, nonprofit professionals can position themselves as credible advocates for their cause, attracting more support and opportunities for collaboration. In the sales world, the concept of relationship management is paramount.

Sales professionals prioritize nurturing and maintaining long-term client relationships to foster loyalty and generate repeat business. Nonprofit fundraisers need to adopt a relationship-centric approach to donor management. Building strong and enduring relationships with donors involves regular communication, expressing appreciation, and providing meaningful engagement opportunities.

By treating donors as valued partners in the nonprofit's mission, fundraisers can cultivate a supportive community that contributes financially through volunteering, advocacy, and spreading the word about the organization's work. Sales skills can be invaluable in the world of fundraising and nonprofit work.

From understanding the needs and motivations of donors to building strong relationships, applying strategic planning, leveraging technology, and upholding ethical practices, the principles and techniques of sales can contribute to the success of fundraising efforts.

By adopting a sales mindset and incorporating sales strategies into their approach, nonprofit professionals can enhance their fundraising effectiveness, raise greater awareness and support for their cause, and ultimately positively impact the communities they serve.

# Chapter 26: How You Can Promote Social Good Beyond Your Professional Life

Salespeople have a unique opportunity to promote social good beyond their professional lives. While their primary focus may be on achieving sales targets and driving business growth, they can also leverage their skills, networks, and influence to impact society positively. One way salespeople can promote social good is through volunteerism and community engagement. By dedicating their time and expertise to local charities, nonprofit organizations, or community initiatives, sales professionals can actively participate in projects that address social issues and improve the lives of others.

This could involve volunteering at food banks, mentoring aspiring entrepreneurs, participating in environmental clean-up drives, or organizing fundraising events for charitable causes. Through their active involvement, salespeople can lend their skills in relationship building, communication, and persuasion to support these organizations in their missions.

Sales professionals often have extensive networks and can reach a wide audience. By leveraging their professional connections, they can share information, stories, and campaigns that shed light on pressing social challenges and encourage others to get involved. This could be through social media posts, blog articles, or speaking engagements where they can inspire others to take action and contribute to meaningful causes.

Salespeople can also participate in corporate social responsibility (CSR) initiatives. Many companies today recognize the importance of giving back to society and have established CSR programs. Sales professionals can actively participate in these initiatives by championing causes, organizing fundraisers, or suggesting partnerships with nonprofit organizations.

By aligning their sales goals with CSR objectives, salespeople can create a positive impact through their efforts and by mobilizing their teams and collaborating with other departments to support social initiatives. Salespeople can use their negotiation skills to facilitate collaborations and partnerships between businesses and social enterprises. They can act as intermediaries, helping companies forge mutually beneficial relationships with nonprofits or social enterprises that share similar values. Through these partnerships, businesses can contribute their resources, expertise to support social projects.

At the same time, salespeople can leverage their negotiation abilities to ensure that these collaborations are sustainable, impactful, and aligned with the interests of all parties involved. Salespeople can contribute to social good by advocating for ethical business practices within their organizations and industries.

By upholding high standards of integrity, transparency, and responsible selling, they can help build trust between businesses and consumers. Sales professionals can educate their colleagues and clients about the importance of ethical conduct, including fair pricing, truthful marketing, and customer-centric practices. By promoting ethical behavior, salespeople can contribute to developing a more socially conscious business environment.

Salespeople can also engage in personal philanthropy by donating a portion of their earnings or engaging in impact investing. They can support social causes and initiatives that resonate with their values, whether education, healthcare, poverty alleviation, or environmental sustainability. By leveraging their financial resources, salespeople can make a direct and tangible impact on the causes they care about, furthering their commitment to social good.

Salespeople can become advocates for social change by actively engaging in public policy discussions and supporting legislation that addresses social issues. They can join industry associations, participate in advocacy groups, or contribute their perspectives to policy debates. Using their knowledge, expertise, and real-world experiences, sales professionals can provide valuable insights to shape policies that promote fairness, inclusivity, and sustainability.

Salespeople can inspire and mentor others to embrace a good social mindset. They can share their stories and lessons learned to motivate and empower their colleagues, clients, and aspiring sales professionals to use their skills and influence for the betterment of society.

By acting as role models, salespeople can encourage others to consider the broader impact of their actions and make conscious choices that contribute to social good. Salespeople can also contribute to social good by leveraging their expertise in sales to provide pro bono consulting or training to nonprofit organizations. Many nonprofits struggle with limited resources and may benefit from sales strategies and techniques to improve their fundraising efforts or enhance their outreach and communication with donors and stakeholders.

By offering their knowledge and skills on a pro bono basis, sales professionals can help nonprofits become more effective in achieving their missions and creating positive social impact. Salespeople can actively engage in social entrepreneurship or intrapreneurship by developing innovative solutions to address social and environmental challenges. They can identify market gaps or underserved communities and develop products or services that generate revenue and contribute to social well-being.

By blending their sales acumen with a social purpose, sales professionals can create sustainable business models that tackle pressing societal issues and create shared value for their customers and communities. Salespeople can also advocate for diversity and inclusion within their organizations and industries.

Promoting a diverse and inclusive sales workforce can foster an environment that values and respects individuals from different backgrounds, perspectives, and experiences. This can lead to greater innovation, collaboration, and understanding and contribute to breaking down barriers and promoting equality both within the sales profession and in society.

Salespeople can be vital in educating and empowering consumers to make socially responsible purchasing decisions. They can provide transparent and accurate information about products and services, including their social and environmental impacts.

By highlighting sustainable and ethical options, sales professionals can help consumers align their purchasing power with their values, encouraging companies to adopt more responsible practices and contributing to a more sustainable marketplace. Salespeople have numerous opportunities to promote social good and make a difference beyond their professional lives.

By providing pro bono consulting, engaging in social entrepreneurship, advocating for diversity and inclusion, empowering consumers, supporting local businesses, prioritizing self-care, leveraging storytelling, and much more, sales professionals can use their skills, influence, and networks to contribute to positive societal change.

By embracing a sales mentality that extends beyond business transactions, salespeople can become agents of social impact, fostering a more compassionate, equitable, and sustainable world.

# Chapter 27: Making Sales and Personal Life More Fulfilling Through Giving Back

Making a positive impact and giving back to others is important in our personal lives and can enhance the fulfilment we experience in our sales careers. Sales professionals have unique opportunities to make a difference through their work and leverage their success to give back to their communities and the causes they care about. Salespeople can make sales and their personal lives more fulfilling by incorporating a philanthropic component into their sales strategies.

Instead of solely focusing on closing deals and generating revenue, sales professionals can align their sales efforts with social impact. They can identify and partner with companies with a strong corporate social responsibility (CSR) focus or support causes that resonate with their values. By promoting products or services with a positive social or environmental impact, salespeople can feel a greater sense of purpose and fulfilment in their sales efforts.

Sales professionals can actively seek out opportunities to volunteer their time and skills to community initiatives. By offering their expertise in sales, such as conducting sales training workshops or mentoring aspiring sales professionals, they can contribute to the development of others and help them achieve their goals. This benefits the individuals they support and provides a sense of personal satisfaction and fulfilment.

Salespeople can also leverage their networks and influence to raise funds or awareness for charitable organizations. They can organize charity events, sponsorships, or donation drives and engage their clients, colleagues, and business partners in these initiatives. By rallying people together for a common cause, sales professionals can foster a sense of community and make a tangible difference in the lives of those in need.

Salespeople can prioritize workplace giving and encourage companies to establish formal giving programs or initiatives. They can advocate for corporate donations, employee volunteer days, or nonprofit partnerships. By creating a culture of giving within their organizations, sales professionals can inspire their colleagues to get involved and make a collective impact on social issues. In their personal lives, sales professionals can also prioritize giving back. They can participate in community service projects, volunteer at local organizations, or engage in fundraising activities for causes they are passionate about.

By actively contributing to their communities, salespeople can forge deeper connections, gain a broader perspective, and experience personal growth. Sales professionals can use their platform and influence to advocate for social change and address important issues. They can speak up about causes they believe in, use social media to raise awareness or engage in public speaking to promote positive change.

By leveraging their sales skills in persuasive communication and relationship-building, they can effectively engage others in conversations that matter and drive meaningful action. Salespeople can make giving back a daily practice by incorporating acts of kindness and generosity into their interactions with clients, colleagues, and strangers. By offering support, encouragement, or assistance to others, they can create a positive ripple effect and contribute to a more compassionate and caring society.

Another way salespeople can make their sales and personal lives more fulfilling is by aligning their values with their professional pursuits. When sales professionals feel connected to the products or services they are selling, they experience a greater sense of purpose and fulfilment. By focusing on industries or products that they are passionate about, salespeople can authentically connect with their customers and have more meaningful interactions.

Sales professionals can also prioritize building strong relationships and connections with their customers. Instead of solely focusing on closing deals, they can take the time to understand their customers' needs and provide personalized solutions.

Salespeople can develop long-term relationships based on trust and mutual respect by actively listening, empathizing, and offering value-added insights. These genuine connections lead to customer loyalty and repeat business and contribute to a more fulfilling sales experience. Sales professionals can seek continuous learning and development opportunities to enhance their sales skills and knowledge.

By investing in their personal growth, they can stay ahead of industry trends, refine their sales techniques, and adapt to evolving customer needs. This commitment to professional growth improves their sales performance and boosts their self-confidence and overall career satisfaction. Salespeople can also strive for a healthy work-life balance to enhance their well-being and satisfaction.

By setting clear boundaries, managing their time effectively, and prioritizing self-care, they can avoid burnout and maintain a fulfilling personal life alongside their sales career. This balance allows them to recharge, pursue their hobbies and interests, and nurture relationships, leading to a more fulfilling and well-rounded life. Sales professionals can embrace a growth mindset and view challenges as opportunities for learning and development.

They can approach them with resilience and determination instead of being discouraged by setbacks or rejections. By reframing setbacks as learning experiences and using them as motivation to improve, salespeople can grow professionally and personally, leading to greater fulfilment in their careers and personal lives.

Sales professionals can actively seek feedback and strive for continuous improvement. By soliciting feedback from their managers, peers, and customers, they can identify areas for growth and make necessary adjustments to their sales approach. This commitment to self-reflection and growth not only leads to better sales performance but also contributes to personal satisfaction and fulfilment.

Salespeople can also take advantage of technology and leverage it to their advantage. By staying updated with the latest sales tools, software, and automation techniques, they can streamline their processes, improve efficiency, and free up more time to focus on meaningful customer interactions. This technology integration enhances their sales effectiveness and allows for a better work-life balance and overall satisfaction.

Sales professionals can foster a positive and supportive work environment by collaborating with their colleagues, sharing knowledge and best practices, and celebrating each other's successes.

By creating a culture of camaraderie and collaboration, salespeople can feel a sense of belonging and support, leading to a more fulfilling and enjoyable work experience.

Sales professionals can make their sales and personal lives more fulfilling by aligning their values with their professional pursuits, building strong relationships, investing in continuous learning, striving for work-life balance, embracing a growth mindset, seeking feedback, leveraging technology, and fostering a positive work environment.

With these strategies in their daily lives, salespeople can experience greater purpose, satisfaction, and fulfilment in their sales careers and personal endeavors.

# Chapter 28: Lessons and Insights from a Life-Lived Sales-First

Throughout a life lived with a sales-first mindset, individuals can gain valuable lessons and insights that extend far beyond the realm of sales. The principles and skills honed in the sales profession can shape personal growth, enhance relationships, and foster overall success and fulfilment. Sales professionals understand the significance of clear and persuasive communication when conveying ideas, building relationships, and influencing others.

This skill translates into personal life, allowing individuals to express themselves more effectively, resolve conflicts, and foster meaningful connections. Salespeople are strangers to rejection and hearing "no" from potential customers. However, they learn to view rejection as a part of the process and an opportunity to learn and improve.

This resilience equally applies to personal life, enabling individuals to bounce back from disappointments, navigate challenges, and persist in pursuing their goals and dreams. Sales professionals also develop strong negotiation skills crucial in business and personal relationships. Negotiation involves finding common ground, understanding the needs and interests of both parties and reaching mutually beneficial agreements.

These skills can be applied to various aspects of personal life, including resolving conflicts, making compromises, and finding win-win solutions in relationships and everyday interactions. A sales-first life teaches individuals the value of empathy and understanding.

Salespeople learn to put themselves in their customers' shoes, empathize with their challenges and concerns, and tailor their approach to meet their needs. This empathetic mindset can be extended to personal relationships, allowing individuals to cultivate deeper connections, show compassion, and support others in need. Sales professionals also recognize the significance of continuous learning and self-improvement.

They understand that staying updated on industry trends, product knowledge, and sales techniques is essential for success. This commitment to growth and learning can also be applied to personal life. Individuals can pursue personal development, expand their knowledge, and acquire new skills to enhance their well-being, relationships, and personal achievements. A sales-first life teaches individuals the importance of building and nurturing networks.

Salespeople understand the power of building strong professional relationships and the benefits of a supportive network. They know they can access valuable resources, opportunities, and insights by fostering connections. Transferring this approach to personal life, individuals can cultivate a diverse network of friends, mentors, and acquaintances who can provide support, guidance, and a sense of community.

Sales professionals also embrace a results-oriented mindset, focusing on setting goals, tracking progress, and driving outcomes. This mindset can be applied to personal life by setting meaningful goals like health, relationships, and personal growth. Individuals can experience a greater sense of purpose, motivation, and fulfilment by taking a proactive approach and measuring progress.

A sales-first life emphasizes the importance of adaptability and resilience in the face of change. Salespeople often encounter shifting market conditions, evolving customer needs, and new competitors. They learn to adapt strategies, embrace change, and find innovative solutions. Applying this mindset to personal life allows individuals to navigate transitions, embrace new opportunities, and thrive in dynamic environments. A sales-first life encourages individuals to embrace a positive mindset and focus on solutions rather than dwelling on problems.

Sales professionals understand the impact of a positive attitude on their success, as it affects their confidence, motivation, and ability to overcome challenges. In personal life, adopting a positive mindset enables individuals to approach obstacles with optimism, find silver linings in difficult situations, and cultivate gratitude for the blessings in their lives.

Living a life with a sales-first mindset brings forth many valuable lessons and insights that have far-reaching implications beyond the realm of sales. The principles and skills honed in the sales profession can shape personal development, enhance relationships, and foster overall happiness and fulfilment.

One key lesson from a sales-first life is the art of building trust. Sales professionals understand the importance of establishing trust with their clients to close deals and foster long-term relationships. They learn to prioritize transparency, integrity, and delivering on promises.

This focus on trust can also be applied to personal life, allowing individuals to cultivate trust with their loved ones, colleagues, and acquaintances. Reliability, honesty, and authenticity can create deeper connections and foster a more harmonious and fulfilling personal life. A sales-first life teaches individuals the importance of problem-solving and finding creative solutions.

Salespeople encounter obstacles and challenges in their professional journeys, such as client objections or intense competition. They develop the ability to think on their feet, identify potential solutions, and adapt their strategies to overcome hurdles. This problem-solving mindset is invaluable in personal life, as it enables individuals to navigate complexities, overcome obstacles, and find innovative approaches to challenges that arise in their personal relationships, careers, and everyday life.

They learn to ask probing questions, actively listen, and empathize with their clients. This skill translates seamlessly into personal life, enhancing relationships and deepening connections. By actively listening to their loved ones, friends, and colleagues, individuals can foster better communication, resolve conflicts more effectively, and cultivate empathy and understanding within their relationships.

A sales-first life encourages continuous learning and self-improvement. Sales professionals understand that the market is ever-evolving, and to stay ahead, they must embrace a growth mindset. They actively seek new knowledge, refine their skills, and stay updated on industry trends.

This commitment to continuous learning can be applied to personal life as well. By embracing lifelong learning, individuals can expand their horizons, explore new interests, and foster personal growth. They can develop new skills, broaden their perspectives, and adapt to the changing dynamics of life with agility and confidence.

A life lived with a sales-first mindset imparts valuable lessons and insights beyond the sales profession. The ability to build trust, solve problems creatively, demonstrate persistence and resilience, listen actively, set and pursue goals, cultivate relationships, foster self-confidence, and embrace continuous learning all contribute to a happier, more successful, and fulfilling personal life.

By integrating these principles and skills into their everyday lives, individuals can unlock their full potential, build meaningful connections, overcome challenges, and thrive in all aspects of life.

# Chapter 29: Applying a Sales Mindset to Lead a Better Everyday Life

Living a better everyday life can be achieved by adopting a sales mindset, which encompasses valuable principles and strategies that extend beyond the realm of sales. By applying the key tenets of the sales profession to various aspects of life, individuals can enhance their personal and professional relationships, improve their problem-solving abilities, and achieve greater success and fulfilment.

Sales professionals excel at identifying their customers' pain points and desires and then offering tailored solutions to address them. Similarly, in everyday life, individuals can benefit from developing a deep understanding of the people around them. By actively listening, empathizing, and seeking to understand the needs and desires of others, individuals can cultivate stronger personal relationships, whether with their family members, friends, colleagues, or even strangers.

This focus on meeting the needs of others fosters connection, trust, and mutual support, leading to a more fulfilling and harmonious everyday life. Sales professionals are skilled communicators who convey their message persuasively and with conviction. Applying this communication prowess to everyday life allows individuals to express themselves effectively, assert their needs, and engage in meaningful conversations. Whether negotiating with a contractor, presenting ideas in a meeting, or resolving conflicts with loved ones, effective communication enhances understanding, resolves misunderstandings, and strengthens relationships.

The sales mindset emphasizes the importance of resilience and a positive attitude in facing challenges. Sales professionals regularly encounter rejection, setbacks, and tough competition, but they understand that persistence and a positive mindset are crucial for success.

Similarly, individuals face various challenges and obstacles in everyday life, whether a career setback, a personal loss, or a health issue. By adopting a resilient mindset and maintaining a positive outlook, individuals can navigate these challenges gracefully, bounce back from setbacks, and find opportunities for growth and learning. This resilience not only helps in overcoming adversity but also inspires and motivates others around them.

A sales mindset encourages individuals to set goals and take proactive steps towards achieving them. Sales professionals are goal-oriented, constantly striving to meet or exceed targets. Applying this mindset to everyday life empowers individuals to set personal goals, whether they are related to career advancement, personal development, health and wellness, or relationships. Individuals create a sense of purpose and direction in their everyday life by setting specific, measurable, achievable, relevant, and time-bound (SMART) goals. They can break down their goals into actionable steps and consistently act towards their desired outcomes.

The sales mindset emphasizes the importance of continuous learning and personal growth. Sales professionals understand that to stay ahead in a competitive market; they must constantly update their knowledge and refine their skills. This dedication to learning can be applied to everyday life by embracing a growth mindset. Individuals can seek personal and professional development opportunities through formal education, self-study, or experiential learning.

By continuously expanding their knowledge and skills, individuals can adapt to changing circumstances, explore new interests, and uncover their full potential. The sales mindset also encourages individuals to develop a strong sense of self-confidence and self-belief. Sales professionals understand that their confidence directly influences their ability to connect with clients, persuade them, and close deals.

Similarly, self-confidence empowers individuals to take risks, embrace new opportunities, and overcome self-doubt in everyday life. By recognizing their strengths, celebrating their accomplishments, and practicing self-care, individuals can cultivate healthy self-esteem and project confidence in all areas of life. Another valuable aspect of the sales mindset is building and maintaining relationships.

Sales professionals understand the importance of nurturing long-term client relationships, as repeat business and referrals are essential for success. Applying this principle to personal life involves investing time and effort in building strong and meaningful relationships with family, friends, mentors, and colleagues. By prioritizing connection, actively listening, and demonstrating genuine care and support, individuals can create a robust support network that enriches their personal life and provides a sense of belonging and fulfilment.

The sales mindset encourages individuals to embrace a problem-solving approach. Sales professionals encounter various challenges, objections, and obstacles during the sales process, and their ability to think creatively and find solutions is crucial for success.

By adopting a problem-solving mindset in everyday life, individuals can approach challenges and setbacks with a solution-oriented attitude. They can identify alternative perspectives, brainstorm innovative ideas, and find practical solutions to their problems. This problem-solving approach enhances resilience, fosters a growth mindset, and paves the way for personal and professional advancement.

Applying a sales mindset to lead a better everyday life involves incorporating the core principles and strategies of the sales profession into various aspects of life. By understanding the needs of others, communicating effectively, cultivating resilience, setting goals, embracing continuous learning, developing self-confidence, building relationships, and adopting a problem-solving approach, individuals can enhance their personal and professional lives.

# Chapter 30: Embracing Sales as a Way of Life

Embracing sales as a way of life goes beyond the boundaries of a career or profession. It entails adopting the core principles, mindset, and sales skills in all aspects of life, from personal relationships to everyday interactions. By incorporating the essence of sales into our daily routines, we can enhance our communication, negotiation, and problem-solving abilities, ultimately leading to a more fulfilling and successful life.

Sales, at its core, is about understanding the needs, desires, and motivations of others. It involves active listening, empathy, and connecting with people more deeply. When we embrace sales as a way of life, we develop the skill of truly listening to others, valuing their perspectives, and understanding their emotions.

This cultivates stronger relationships, fosters trust and mutual respect, and enables us to navigate various social situations with grace and empathy. Sales teach us the art of persuasion. Persuasion is not about manipulating or forcing others to agree with you but rather about effectively communicating our ideas, beliefs, and values compellingly.

When we embrace sales as a way of life, we learn to express ourselves clearly and persuasively while respecting the autonomy and opinions of others. This skill can benefit us in personal relationships, allowing us to effectively articulate our needs, resolve conflicts, and collaborate with others to achieve mutually beneficial outcomes.

Sales also emphasize the importance of problem-solving. Sales professionals encounter challenges and objections regularly, and their success hinges on their ability to find creative solutions. When we adopt a sales mindset in our personal lives, we develop the skill of approaching problems with a solution-oriented attitude.

We become adept at identifying alternative perspectives, brainstorming innovative ideas, and finding practical solutions to our obstacles. This problem-solving approach empowers us to overcome setbacks, embrace change, and navigate the complexities of life with resilience and resourcefulness. Sales encourage continuous learning and personal growth.

Successful sales professionals understand that staying ahead of the competition requires ongoing self-improvement and staying up-to-date with industry trends. When we embrace sales as a way of life, we become lifelong learners seeking personal and professional development opportunities.

We engage in self-reflection, identify areas for improvement, and actively seek knowledge and experiences that expand our horizons. This commitment to growth enhances our skills and knowledge and fuels our personal fulfilment and sense of purpose. Sales teach us the value of perseverance and resilience.

Sales professionals regularly face rejection and setbacks but understand that persistence is key to achieving their goals. When we embrace sales as a way of life, we adopt a resilient mindset that allows us to bounce back from failures, learn from our mistakes, and keep moving forward. This resilience extends beyond sales-related challenges and equips us to navigate the ups and downs of life with determination and optimism. Sales emphasize the importance of goal setting and planning.

Sales professionals set clear targets and develop strategies to achieve them. Embracing sales as a way of life encourages us to set meaningful goals in all areas of life, whether they are related to career, personal growth, relationships, health, or financial well-being.

By setting specific, actionable goals and creating a plan to attain them, we gain clarity, motivation, and a sense of direction in our everyday life. Embracing sales as a way of life means cultivating a positive and service-oriented mindset. Sales professionals understand that their success is intrinsically linked to their ability to provide value to their customers. We seek opportunities to be of service, offer assistance, and make a difference in the lives of those around us.

This mindset fosters a sense of fulfilment, purpose, and interconnectedness, enhancing our relationships and impact on the world. Embracing sales as a way of life entails integrating the principles and skills of sales into all aspects of our existence. By understanding the needs of others, developing persuasive communication skills, embracing problem-solving, committing to continuous learning, cultivating resilience, setting goals, and adopting a positive and service-oriented mindset, we can lead a more fulfilling and successful life.

Embracing sales as a way of life empowers us to navigate challenges, build meaningful connections, achieve our aspirations, and positively impact the world. Embracing sales as a way of life encourages us to adopt a proactive approach to personal growth and success. Sales professionals have driven individuals who actively seek opportunities, take the initiative, and seize the moment.

When we embrace sales as a way of life, we become more proactive in pursuing our dreams and aspirations. We understand that success doesn't come by waiting for opportunities to come to us but by actively seeking and creating them.

This proactive mindset empowers us to take charge of our personal and professional lives, making intentional choices and taking calculated risks to achieve our goals. Embracing a sales mindset in our personal lives can significantly improve our financial well-being. Sales professionals are skilled in managing their finances, understanding the value of their products or services, and effectively communicating that value to potential customers.

When we adopt a sales mindset, we become more mindful of our spending habits, prioritize financial planning, and develop a keen sense of value. We become better equipped to make informed decisions about our investments, savings, and expenses, improving financial stability and a more secure future. Embracing sales as a way of life reminds us of the importance of building and nurturing a strong network of connections. Sales professionals understand the value of building relationships, establishing rapport, and maintaining long-term partnerships.

When we adopt a sales mindset, we become more intentional in cultivating and nurturing our personal and professional networks. We recognize the power of collaboration, the benefits of seeking support from others, and the value of giving and receiving feedback.

This focus on relationship-building enhances our personal and social lives, expanding our opportunities and creating a supportive network of individuals who share our values and aspirations. Embracing sales as a way of life extends beyond a career or profession. It encompasses a mindset of continuous growth, proactive action, financial savvy, adaptability, leadership, a strong work ethic, a commitment to excellence, and relationship-building.

By embracing sales principles in our personal lives, we can cultivate personal and professional success, lead a more fulfilling and purposeful life, and positively impact the world around us. Embracing sales as a way of life is about embracing a mindset of growth, resilience, and an unwavering belief in our ability to create positive change and achieve our highest aspirations.